Overcoming
WARFARE
In the
WORKPLACE
A BIBLICAL PERSPECTIVE

DR. BRENDA BANNISTER

BBMF Inc.

PO Box 15115

Ft. Lauderdale, Florida 33318

kingdomwealthdistributor@gmail.com

Ordering Information:

Quantity sales. Special discounts are available on quantity purchases by corporations, associations, and others. For details, contact the publisher at the address above.

Layout assisted by www.diverseskillscenter.com/ P.O. Box 290963/ Tampa, FL 33687

Printed in the United States of America

Library of Congress Cataloging - No. 2019909519

Overcoming Warfare in the Workplace ISBN – 978-1-64633-137-6 (paperback)

DEDICATION

It is with great honor and pleasure that I dedicate this blessing of my first writing project to my dearest husband, Ernest.

To Ernest

Indeed, you are the gift from God to me and our family who makes me feel incredibly blessed and grateful every day. I appreciate the multitude of ways you've shown your love, support and commitment in encouraging me every step of the way to finish strong in the completion of this task. Thank you for being my counselor, my comrade, and my partner in this life.

You are most significant to me and my heart thanks to God for you.

ENDORSEMENTS

There are many books on spiritual warfare, and I thank God that every one of them is needed.

However, I believe that this book on; "Overcoming Warfare in the Workplace", is what's needed now in the body of Christ, for those who are in the workplace or in ministerial work.

I can see believers being stirred up and becoming more sharper in their gift of discernment and becoming more aware of spiritual rulers. I believe Intercessors will begin to understand how to pray from the greater place in the anointing and to dismantle every stronghold. What a time for a book such as this.

Apostle Carolyn Bradshaw,
Last Call for Jesus Ministry
Hollywood, Florida

There are many books on the topic of "Warfare" but not many people who actually experienced it and came out with the VICTORY.
Dr. Bannister has, is and will continue to not only experience warfare but she comes out victoriously because of her faith in our "Lord of Host" who is the Lord of the armies, her prayer life and her determination to come out with a great testimony.
Reading her journey is like having a map going into uncharted territory. One of the assurances is you gain knowledge of whom and what you are up against, giving you the ability to fight with dignity and honor, because of the GOD we serve. Enjoy, learn and activate the jewels of wisdom that are expressed in this remarkable book.

All for His glory,
Prophetess Sharon J. Boykin

Dr. Brenda Bannister, a woman of prayer, precision and purpose. This leader is fully equipped to birth such a book. Her experience in the workforce has catapulted her into dimensions of prayer which enabled her to become an overcomer in this realm. I recommend that everyone regardless of religious preference read and glean from this book. This must read, will allow those experiencing insurmountable resistance in the workforce to overcome the difficulties as they go about their earthed assignments.

Prophet Rose Ann Greaves

Dr. Brenda Bannister is a prolific prayer intercessor and warfare strategists. Her spiritual journey is strategic in nature, as she is commissioned by God. Her platform to enforce the kingdom in the workforce has allowed her to reach all humanity regardless of religious preference.

She embodies Gods Governmental principals which she now imparts through this Masterpiece. I believe this manual will effect positive change and balance in the workforce. Dr. Bannister is truly an ambassador of intercession and clinical leadership.

Ambassador Dr. Megan Massay
MM International

TABLE OF CONTENTS

FOREWORD

Don't depend on the enemy not coming; depend rather on being READY for him.

-Sun Tzu

Military operations General Sun Tzu has been an ancient sanctuary of wisdom for warfare throughout the ages and civilizations of all time. We have all been made subject to the influence of WAR in some way, shape, form or fashion. In many cases we have been both the victim and the villain as we are often contributing factors to the harsh environments, we have been made subject to. Every now and then, in life, we will find ourselves enlisted as ground soldiers in battles that will require spiritual engagement to undo the strongholds of spiritual entanglements.

God gives his toughest battles to his strongest soldiers. I believe that God has raised up voices like Dr. Brenda Bannister to shine the light on a hidden network of warfare that many believers will face in their lifetime. The Bible says that the enemy is the Prince of the "power" of the air. Satan, when coming to tempt Jesus on the mountain was able to offer him the kingdoms of the world which shows us that he has in many ways taken possession of them. The marketplace is a mountain, so therefore within this it is HIGHLY likely that you will face the enemy in these fields.

The Bible says "My people perish for a lack of knowledge" Hosea 4:6. Knowledge leads to power which is something every opponent fear! "Overcoming Warfare in the Workplace," is a study guide that maps out victories for every scenario of warfare possible. By way of experience and revelation from God, Dr.

Brenda Bannister decodes powerful truths that will render the enemy's plots and plans useless and ineffective against you.

Understand that hell's toxic trio has always been with this mandate: to kill, steal and destroy! However, we have been given power over the enemy to subdue every kingdom. This book will teach you how to subdue the enemy by reason in studying his strategies and tactics. "If you know the enemy and know yourself you need not fear the results of a hundred battles." – Sun Tzu

Apostle Cierra L. Jones   *ACLJ Worldwide Ministries*

PREFACE

In preparing to minister at an event: "Pulling Down Strongholds", I began meditating on scriptures relating to spiritual warfare, studying different translations, and researching various sources.

In January 2019, as I began to focus in on the subject matter scheduled for mid-March, I began receiving spiritual downloads of revelatory knowledge on this vast subject. More and more my heart was filled with anticipation to share the discovery of these hidden truths.

A little more than a month into my studies I suffered a broken ankle in three places, had surgery, sutures on both the inside and outside of the foot and was confined to a wheelchair with no weight-bearing restrictions which would last throughout the scheduled speaking engagement.

Overcoming the warfare and opposition, I kept preparing for the event hoping to receive medical clearance to be able to bear enough weight on my foot to stand and minister by the time of the actual event.

Fourteen days away from the event, the doctor removed the sutures, but did not provide medical clearance.

I was given a knee walker and a boot to aid in the support of the leg but remained unable to bear any weight on the foot. I remained confined. Although disappointed, none the less, I was still trying to decipher a way to accomplish this assignment.

After sharing my heart with a dear woman of God, she said to me: "I know you're used to being up and moving around as you minister; but the Lord is saying "Go Forward," There may be a boot on your foot but it's not on your mouth. So even if you gotta preach from the wheelchair. You just release the Word of the Lord and leave the rest to Him."

Reignited to continue, two days later the event host informed me that my initial date and time slot had already been filled. Nonetheless, I had been replaced. Let me just encourage someone right here who maybe facing some type of physical challenge reserved to handicap you or an injustice set to deter you...... "Persevere through with the right disposition. How is your attitude, or temperament? Is your character still intact? God takes notice of your disposition during the distance – during the testing of disappointments.

The enemy will always attempt to drown out the voice of God as we are seeking guidance and direction.

Overcoming the Warfare entails the process of silencing the negativity of the demonic whispers. The Lord began to impress upon me to transfer the following wealth of knowledge and three decades of ministerial and work experience into book form.

Finally, I was being released to expose the culprit working behind the scenes in our personal lives and particularly within the workplace environment where such hostility is becoming ever more blatant. It is imperative that we as believers know how to respond when we are lambasted by attacks from the enemy. Each page turned by its reader is a dagger into the diabolical plan of the enemy as this resource provides both a spiritual and practical side to achieving overall victory.

I will also extract pivotal examples from the Biblical lifestyles of Nehemiah, Daniel, Joshua, Moses, and others exemplifying character traits of leadership undergoing various challenges and oppositions.

We will discover how to prophetically unmask the strategies of the enemy in the workplace as well as in our individual lives to free ourselves from his devices and thus we will learn how to live a life of power from the throne of God Himself.

This resource will be the cornerstone for both current and future employees, and the myriad of leaders abroad serving to gain an advantage in overcoming spiritual warfare tactics.

I am blessed with this window of opportunity to have penned this project with the fingerprint of God on a subject that is not widely ministered on but affects so many of us in the workplace. Certainly, what the enemy meant to use for my destruction and downfall, God has used for my good and His Glory in reclaiming spiritual territory in the penning of this book. Know that this movement is about territory. For the kingdoms of this world shall become the Kingdoms of our God.

"Rejoice not over me, O my enemy; when I fall, I shall rise; when I sit in darkness, the Lord will be a light to me" (Micah 7:8)

ACKNOWLEDGEMENTS

First and foremost, I thank the Lord for enabling a dream come true and that with Him all things are possible. I thought this dream of writing a book was impossible, especially due to my busy work schedule. The events that led up to this project were peculiar to say the least; but GOD!

The Holy Spirit, who teaches me all things that are true; provided me with a supernatural grace, peace and strength in the fulfillment of this task.

I acknowledge and thank my husband, **Ernest**, for his loving support and always believing in me. The encouragement he's given me has pushed me to pursue this passion; even in the midst of a medical challenge *(broken ankle)* Hats off to him as he has provided me with exceptional care all while serving as my personal chauffeur during this entire ordeal. Since this undertaking, his extraordinary patience and unselfishness has proven remarkable, considering having to often miss home cooked meals, maintaining housekeeping chores and enduring my "all-nighters" at the computer. I'm grateful for everything you are, and "the many hats you wear" in doing all that you do.

Thank you, Honey.

I'm also very grateful to both of my amazing, brilliant, lovely daughters, **Brenique** and **Brenisha**, for patiently supporting me through the writing process of this project. Whenever I felt tensed and overwhelmed with thoughts that I couldn't make it through an assignment, they somehow always knew the exact family fun get-a-way that was needed. Thank you both for the perfect "relaxing venues" while also providing spiritual nourishment with seasoned words of encouragement and wisdom. Indeed, you are forever my precious gems.

Thank you, best friends.

I would also like to deeply thank my mother **Ida** and auntie-mama **Ellies** who have been my biggest behind the scene cheerleaders. They have provided me with a level of inspiration of which I will be forever grateful. Thank you, family, for your listening ears and shoulders to lean on when I encountered times of enormous frustration.

Writing a book without any training has created a huge learning curve for me. Kimberlaine Johnson, of Queen B Publications and Tam Jernigan, editor of Publisher Chick Editing has patiently assisted me professionally with numerous questions and concerns. I however cannot thank enough Publisher and Prophetess Cynthia Johnson of Diverse Skills Center. A hidden treasure revealed in the essence of a precious gem. Indeed, she have served honorable as a "ram in the bush", and a warfare strategist in accompanying me in the release of this project. Last but certainly not least; I'd like to extend a special honor to my Apostle and spiritual mother Cierra LaShaun Jones. "An authentic gift from God". From the beginning stages of this project, she has served both as a master generalist and a birthing specialist in providing me the necessary support and "strong push" that has produced favorable results. I am forever grateful.

I thank each of you for all the shared resources, contributions, encouragement and useful critiques of this project.

Blessings to all!

CHAPTER 1

MY POSTAL "VIBE"

I began my postal career in 1987 as a letter carrier. Contrary to what some might think, delivering mail is not easy and there is a sharp learning curve. Dogs, weather (record-breaking heat, rainstorms, blizzards, frosty winter times) and darkness (nighttime mail delivery which can have serious, lethal consequences) are just a few challenges of a Letter Carrier. My first assigned delivery unit was comprised of 90% walking routes. Quite naturally, dogs were my most frequent dangerous encounter.

In 1993, I was promoted Customer Service Supervisor in delivery operations in a fairly competitive environment. My knowledge of postal operations in carrier and finance stations rapidly enhanced as I often accepted challenges to work in the fairly large, complex facilities.

The workforce in my working facilities have all been very diverse and I have held various leadership positions throughout my thirty-two years of service.

I've witnessed some of the challenges of this fast paced, changing industry. It has become significantly more demanding over the past ten years. This is more than likely why many of my peers from other locations candidly express an enormous amount of responsibility placed on their shoulders daily, and the verbal browbeating and intimidation of upper management has caused high stress levels.

In retrospect, a small loss in the scheme of things that are missing from our corporate jobs is the inability or the means to control and manage within the parameters of our accountability. Windows of opportunity or favorable circumstances are also limited within the scope of broadening skills that already exist.

- We are without control over our day-to-day.
- We are not developing skills that we value.

However, for the most part, I've been favored to work with pretty decent managers throughout the years and my job overall with the USPS has been both challenging and rewarding. I'm truly grateful for my postal experience as it has served as an excellent means of living and the learning processes have guided me throughout life's journey.

Most of the greatest challenges and revelations I share with you came in the context of God forcing truth on me in learning more on spiritual warfare at an intense level. All of which was done from a platform of prayer.

I'd now like to park it here for a moment to take you behind the scenes into a delivery unit by way of a few employees' reviews found on multiple websites. This is a key list of personal views from employees around the globe to help you gain a better perspective of a union environment within the delivery culture; particularly as it relates to "my typical workdays" outlined in the forth coming chapters.

PARKED AT THE POST OFFICE

- "I created lasting relationships."
- "A very fast paced environment."
- "Underlying pressures."
- "They treat you like a body and not a person."
- "Sometimes common sense is not the norm."
- "Every day is a new adventure."
- "Each day it was a challenge to distribute all mail, cover routes, and keep all customers satisfied. It was difficult but exhilarating at the same time. Very rewarding."
- "No work/life balance unrealistic expectations."

- "The Postal Service as a whole is not necessarily a horrible place to work; however, the work culture / ethics have changed tremendously! There is no value or postal pride anymore. There is no accountability for lost items, keys. I could go on and on."
- "Great Benefits and advancement opportunities."
- "USPS is a 24/7 operation with employees working sixty plus hours weekly."
- "Hardly any time for family or self."
- "Lots to do every day and it's never the same thing! Every day is unique with its challenging Situations."
- "Great job security and career potential."
- "No two days are the same."
- "Most favorable reviews of former supervisors' states: Great Benefits."
- "Relentless stress at high level positions."
- "Cons = Unions."
- "Upholding company's policies with the union undermining tactics."
- "Upper Level micromanagement."
- "The stress eats away at people."

- "The fact the union making it next to impossible to be fired causes a low work ethic in nearly all employees. Additionally, as a postal supervisor the lack of reward is added by constantly being yelled and threatened."

- "Very stressful and demanding with completing my task within a certain time frame every day."

- "What I hated most about the 204B job was constant micro-managing from upstairs."

- "It's hard to make anything of a job when you aren't given any leeway to do so. Constant obsession with mostly irrelevant statistical data is the downfall of this organization."

- "I know quite well from management's perspective this is a stressful, mostly thankless job."

"Since moving into a management position for the last 12 years I have gained a much better understanding of the workings of our upper management structure and that understanding does not change much about what has already been expressed...except... there are always sides to every problem. My peers and I all agree that the carrier supervisor position, which most 204-Bs operate within, is, without question, the worst job in the USPS. You are overworked and under appreciated by your boss, and you are reviled and ridiculed by those you are tasked to manage. There is no "Win" in that position. For my entire career I have observed those "Few" who make life impossible for the many and especially so for that middle-manager who has to deal directly with the day in and day out. I have loved and hated my many jobs over the years, but I can honestly say that the job will always be what you make it."

"When I started 12 years ago as a city carrier, we had routes that were bigger. Had more mail volume, more stops, cased all of our mail, handled all change of address card and took pride in "owning our routes!" Now we have DPS – Delivery Point Sequence. It's a mail sorting process that puts the mail for carrier routes into delivery order. "It sorts 60% of our mail, we can't view change of address cards, and the only thing that management worries about is MSP scans or whatever deems the flavor of the month". MSP is Managed Service Points – A program intended to improve the time of day consistency of mail delivery to customers.

"The unions are the biggest impediment to getting the job done. They refuse to embrace new ideas and go out of their way to protect the most unproductive, belligerent members. I don't know how management can function and get their job done."

"The USPS has a vast uneducated managerial staff in lower and upper management ranks. Education plays NO role in promoting USPS supervisors which is a direct cause to the root problem of a very poor work environment. Give the USPS management and supervisors a standard test to be promoted workers. Supervisors are rarely in the unit and show no interest in supervising the work product."

DRESSED FOR WORK AND WAR

Each day as I walked into the workplace, I felt like a warrior dressed for battle, walking onto a battlefield of a war zone. It similarly mocks the basic floor plan within a delivery unit of carriers and route cases as they encircle the supervisor's workstation; each waiting his or her turn to skirmish.

The ratio of 1 supervisor monitoring 55-75 employees on a norm in this specific setting seems irrational but is not uncommon in the postal world.

My primary function was to oversee the daily operations of the clerk and letter carrier craft employees within a delivery unit, as well as motivating, inspiring, guiding and encouraging employees to rise to a higher level of productivity. Educating and training new employees and newly promoted supervisors were also all within the scope of my responsibilities.

The job of supervising employees in a unionized environment has its own unique set of rules and challenges. The company still controls the work environment in this special framework; however, understanding the very particular principles of the union environment will be key to success. Nonetheless, these are basic leadership principles that apply equally to any work setting.

My workplace perspective for a little over a decade was that of me as a warrior standing at a stand-up computer desk located in the middle of a fiery furnace surrounded by ferocious lions. The lions depict the various kinds of complex and challenging personalities that I encountered daily. They were vicious, slothful, undermining, backbiting, and confrontational to say the least. Of course, this does not sum up the total workforce in which I supervised. Actually, the majority of the workforce were courteous, diligent, and knowledgeable with honorable work ethics. However, for the purpose of this warfare assignment, we will view the former in an attempt to heighten your awareness in identifying and exposing the hidden tactics and agendas as it relates to spiritual warfare in the workplace and/or within your specific sphere of influence.

I'd like now to mainly focus on scenarios and experiences of warfare encountered in the workplace of the past 10-12 years where I've professionally served in the leadership capacity as an AM Customer Service Supervisor.

Undoubtedly, the Lord provided me this platform with a two-fold mission; to develop my character in displaying the Fruit of the Spirit and for the training and developing my overall skills; particularly in the art of spiritual warfare.

Isaiah 43:2-3 &5 and Psalm 23:4 was my initial-level WORD to stand on at the commencement of this assignment.

"When you go through deep waters and great trouble, I will be with you. When you go through rivers of difficulty, you will not drown! When you walk through the fire of oppression, you will not be burned up; the flames will not consume you. For I am the Lord your God, the Holy One of Israel...Do not be afraid, for I am with you." (Isaiah 43:2-3 & 5 NLT)."

This Scripture is so powerful when you're either in a trial or sense that you're heading towards one. This is God showing you through His Word that no matter what He allows you to go through, and no matter how heavy the weight of the trial may be,

He will be with you. And not only that, but it won't be so strong that you can't handle it. It will not overtake you.

Also, in **Psalm 23:4** the Psalmist says, *"Yea though I walk through the valley of the shadow of death, I will fear no evil, for you are with me: your rod and your staff, they comfort me."*

There are some struggles God will bring us over, there are some He will bring us under, there are some we simply have to walk through. But rest to assured, He will never send us anywhere that He won't accompany us.

MY WORKDAY

My typical workday begins between 2:30am or 3:00am in prayer. During my consecrated fellowship with the Lord – I find its always a different experience as you learn to yield to the moving of the Holy Spirit.

These divine encounters are expressively revealing, refining, refreshing and reinvigorating. I always dread nearing the climax of each encounter; having to leave the sweet fellowship with the Father to get dressed for work. It seems unfair. There is usually a sweet melody or a hymn of a song which arises from within my spirit and lingers as I'm preparing for work. Everything feels just right. I sense gratefulness of heart with recharged faith for the day ahead. I am still on a high, worshiping God all the way to work while it is, yet the dawning of the day and the dew is still on the roses. I've consecrated my day, I've commanded my morning, faith has been stirred, revelation is flowing, everything is better than ok.

Normally, around 5 a.m. when I arrived at work, there is about 5% of the employees there, who are scheduled for this time frame. The work floor is relatively noisy with sounds of mail machines, rolling equipment, music, and loud conversations. The majority of the workforce of carriers report approximately three hours later. Quite naturally, the noise level is escalated even higher with the ringing of the office phones, while smartphones are constantly beeping and pinging alerts. The strategy of the enemy at all cost is to ensnare us in the "sound" which creates an atmosphere of confusion around us.

I'm aware of a mood swing as I began to walk about the workroom floor to review the previous day's findings and reports.

My posture is changing from one of praise and thanksgiving to one filled with questions and stress.

- Now, why didn't carrier A return on time?
- Why did carrier B run-over the authorized time?
- OMG, they had to send the cavalry out to help carrier C again?
- I don't believe the same vehicles keep breaking down!

- Why can't the vehicle maintenance department repair the vehicles on the first try?

And the list goes on and on.

I am quite aware that my spiritual high that I felt during my devotion is now slowly fading away. And about thirty minutes after 90% workforce of carriers clock in - it is nearly gone and resentment attempts to replace my peace and power. Although my focus is now completely on the work at hand; I'm never depleted in my spirit. Throughout the chaotic work climate, I continue to sense the gentle nudging of the Holy Spirit guiding me in decision making, handling employee confrontations and customer issues throughout my day.

What happened to me? A sudden disagreement or rude word from someone else's nasty disposition no doubt inspired and produced by iniquity just reached out and touched me. That is just how quick the worshipful experience is drowned out and replaced with an escalated level of blood pressure. If you're not fully armed, you can become the victim of an argument, part of Satan's psychological warfare in manipulating and managing your mind to distract you. His strategy is to put pressure on you from every side.

For years I've worked with individuals unvaryingly in the day-to-day task of priding themselves in heated disagreements, bickering, arguing, and engaging in angry undercurrents. The Bible teaches us as servants of the Lord that we must not get up in strife (2 Timothy 2:23-24). It says we are not to have anything to do with trifling (ill-informed, unedifying, stupid) controversies over ignorant questionings because they foster strife and breed quarrels. I've found in leadership that such avoidance is not always practicable. A level of accountability lies within our scope of responsibility to address issues of this nature.

To overcome the warfare of keeping conflict and discord out of your life, you'll have to purposely practice diffusing conversations that lead to distress and turmoil of the soul. Choose to respond with a soft answer that turns away wrath (Proverbs 15:1) or choose just to squash it. Just think about it, why would I entertain the idea that even though I think I'm right, there's a possibility I'm wrong. We can cause all kinds of problems just by trying to prove we are right, and what good does it really do in the end? It only satisfies the flesh; and the Bible says, *"those controlled by the flesh cannot please God." (Romans 8:8)*

CHAPTER 2

LEADING WITH A STYLE OF SIMPLICITY

THE CLASS OF LEADERSHIP - (Leadership Assessment I)

EXTREME STYLES OF LEADERSHIP –
WHAT'S YOUR PREFERENCE?

I've been working since I was thirteen, and my various bosses run the gamut from wonderful leaders to imperious dictators. The man or woman in charge ought to be humbled by their position and take seriously the weight of their influence. All of which to say, there's a big difference between leadership and management. Not all managers are leaders. I've been told that you cannot be an effective boss by being a friend to those one supervises. I have some serious concerns about this as I personally feel that being a friend at work is a good way to gain employee confidence and performance.

I have found that some people prefer bottom line results over anything else. They value quantity and achieving performance standards at all expense. However, predefined measures or performance indicators should not solely constitute a company's' metric of numbers for analysis and evaluation.

They felt they could be candid or courteous, but not both. Those who mastered crucial conversations found the "and."

31

They learned how to be candid and courteous. And so, it is with managing or leading. In this segment, I'll try to help you see that you can be fair, friendly and be a boss. First of all, you cannot effectively lead in either of the extreme styles of leadership. There must be balance.

I've extracted from various style of leaders and sources of leadership that the elite class of high achievers are careful not to fall into the mold of choosing one means to an end. Instead they achieve a balance consisting of merging results and a peaceful coexistence. They value getting results and getting along. They establish their high expectations and motivate their team in desiring to produce quality results. This is reflective of the elite class of leaders that have discovered a way to engage with employees candidly while also being courteous and respectful.

I've often been told by my employees about my ability to be compassionate and caring; while tolerating "no nonsense". I'm reminded of an instance whereby one of the carriers (06) said to me: "You know what I really like about you? Over the years, I've watched your consistency in being firm with me and others in confronting our performance and behavior; and yet, you never hold a grudge. You will firmly make your point about what has to be said or done on Monday, and Tuesday always begins anew." This speaks volume as to mastering the skill of Balancing Authority "and" Compassion.

So, here is some specific advice to help you find your "and." Don't let your friendliness slide into incompletion of your workload, missing deadlines, exceeding budget hours, or not holding people accountable. Don't let your firm management style slide into not involving engaging or giving recognition. The choice is yours. I'm a believer in the power of the word "and." Taking the time and energy to find the "and" is my choice! Regardless of our preferred style of leadership – Exemplify professionalism at all times!

THE CLASS OF LEADERSHIP - (Leadership Assessment II)

KNOW YOUR UNIQUE PLACE – WHAT'S YOUR CAPACITY?

God has chosen you to lead in some capacity. Whether it's a people, or a project, the capacity of leadership varies.

To be a leader, you don't have to be an elected official or a CEO. Whether in day-to-day life, at school, or in the workplace, a leader is someone who provides example, guidance, and direction. A fancy title doesn't make someone a true leader; rather qualities and actions do.

Fathers and mothers must lead, older children must lead younger children, employers lead employees who must lead other employees. We all find ourselves on the chain of authority, and submission is the name of the game! No matter who you are leading, there is always someone who is in authority over you. Ultimately, your authority is the Lord Jesus Christ. He cares about every area of leadership he gives us. Romans 13:1b says, "for there is no authority except that which God has established." Therefore, whatever area of influence God has given us, He requires us to be good stewards in it.

We are not all called to have the same identical challenges, burdens, visions, job assignments. However, we all do have a part in the plan of God. Don't leave your educator's position just to acquire a business partner in selling real estate or don't put all your eggs in one basket to pursue music just because your friend Yogi is doing it. The challenge is being able to discern your unique place.

It is critical that you understand the boundaries and perimeters of your gifts, talents, and your callings. Knowing your limitations is just as important as knowing all of your potential. As long as you stay within your boundaries, exactly in the place where God has ordained you to be, it doesn't matter how ferocious looking the devil appears or how great the obstacles appear to be, you have a promise of divine protection and provision!

If you are called to a supervisor's position and you do it comfortably and with great ease, but others have compelled you to advance to an upper management's position where you are miserable, then go back to doing what you were called and gifted to do. That was me once upon a time, but I've found blessing and contentment will come when you get back to the place God wants you to be. Then everything will be restored into divine alignment.

THE CLASS OF LEADERSHIP - (Leadership Assessment III)

SUCCESS

In business, nobody achieves success entirely on their own. No man is an island. Business is about relationships, which is why it's so important to make time to build them. Focus on cultivating relationships with coworkers and industry colleagues in all areas of the business. In the future, you will need those people either because you need their specific expertise or simply as a friend. This industry has many peaks and valleys, and very few of us have gotten through the valleys without a little help from others.

You can be sure that when an opportunity opens up, the relationships you cultivate will be an important factor in your ability to level up. The truth about the so-called ladder of success is that there really isn't one, and even if there was one, it would look different to each person.

✓ Procrastination is a major backlash and one of the worst traits to imbibe in achieving success.

✓ Always be on the move to achieve your goals.

✓ There is no perfect path to success; so, stop giving excuses about why you're not doing anything! There is no success without sacrifice – Every person who has achieved any success in life has made sacrifices to do so. Effective leaders sacrifice much that is good in order to dedicate themselves to what is best.

It is often reported that the people who get ahead in the corporate world aren't those who are best at their jobs, but those who are good at politics and 'playing the game'. We tend to hear as of a result: "That's 'just life". Do appearances, perceptions and presentation carry more weight than output and execution?

Refuse to let your career life define you, so you won't be left to contend with whether you like yourself defined that way or not. That, I think, is what makes corporate jobs frustrating and alarming. I don't want to be defined by my "nice career wear or by stylish threads and designer pumps". More importantly, I'd rather be secured in knowing that my identity is solidified in Christ. Thus, it is not necessary to sacrifice authenticity for ambition.

Success in leadership is comprised of or embodies the following simple key components or indicators.

Requirements for Successful Leadership

◆ Be courteous and polite - While there are other factors that influence your ability to gain respect, such as work ethic, personal character and attitude. One thing is for sure, you must give respect in order to deem or be respected.

◆ Practice empathy and compassion - To understand how to respect other people, put yourself in their shoes and attempt to truly understand where they're coming from. True respect stems from a deep sense of empathy. Respecting each other is a way of getting along and making the world livable and more delightful for everyone.

◆ You must be found trustworthy - As an immediate, hands-on supervisor I was privy to a lot of my employees' personal matters as they expressed the concern of their hearts in confidence to me. When employees encounter unexpected, unfortunate situations outside of work (and everyone does sooner or later) I would check in on my employees (often outside of work hours) offering support, encouragement or just a listening ear. Contrary to belief, you do not undermine your authority by caring!

◆ Must possess ability to challenge: Leaders are those that challenge the status quo. They have their own style of doing things and problem-solving and are usually the ones who think outside the box.

◆ Don't abuse your power – As a leader of authority, "Never expect others to defer to you "just because".

◆ Be willing to accept feedback. Each of us have blind spots that must be dealt with, and you may not recognize them unless someone points them out to you. Being in charge does not mean you're perfect or that the buck stops with you. If you can't handle constructive criticism - you probably shouldn't be in a leadership role.

◆ Reinforce Recognition - It's important to make employees feel valued, and on a more basic level – noticed. It also reinforces the fact that their contribution matters and expresses gratitude for their hard work, which encourages them to continue working hard. Without employees succeeding on an individual level, the business as a whole can't succeed either. It's one thing to acknowledge the importance of employee success and quite another thing to enable it. This is a challenge that organizations of all sizes, locations, and industries face.

THE CLASS OF LEADERSHIP - (Leadership Assessment IV)

- PREPARATION/PLAN AHEAD
- ADDING VALUE
- RESPECT
- HONOR

The above key indicators are the most predominantly used by me in achieving overall effectiveness in leadership. These qualities have also proven effective in cultivating a hostile-free workplace.

The Law of Navigation is preparation. When you prepare well, you convey confidence and trust to people. Leaders who are good navigators are capable of equipping and empowering others on a journey of a lifetime. The original acrostic by John Maxwell inspired me to create my very own extensive version:

- **P**redetermine a course of action in Purposeful *PRAYER*

- **L**ay out your goals in *LOVE*

- **A**djust your priorities in *ACCURACY*

- **N**otify key players with confidence and in *NOBILITY*

- **A**llow time or acceptance before moving abruptly in *ACTION*

- **H**ead into action in *Humility*.

- **E**xpect challenges to be overcome in *EFFICIENCY & EXPERIENCE*

- **A**lways point to "THE SOURCE" of all successes in *ADORATION*

- **D**aily review your plan with discernment and in *DILIGENCE*

The Law of Addition is adding value by serving others. The one who leads is no more important than the person who faithfully serves in obscurity. It is not the position that adds value to us as people. We were created with value and worth.

"Adding Value as a Distributor of Wealth" was the brand given to me by the LORD in 2007 by way of a dream. I immediately began intricately weaving this identifying mark into the fabric of my lifestyle. It is a core value; not only in the aspect of leadership but as a lifestyle principle.

The bottom line in workplace leadership is the attitude of the leader which affects the atmosphere of the office. If you desire to add value by serving others, you will become a better leader. Your employees will achieve more, develop more loyalty, and have a better time getting things done than you ever thought possible. That's the power of the Law of Addition.

God created all people and created them differently for reasons and purpose we may not understand. Regardless of how we perceive other people to be, they are God's creations, and it's God's will for us to show respect to everyone.

Leading with Respect

◆ **Respect Yours**elf -You are an important person and you deserve to be treated well. You'll then be able to help others effectively.

◆ **Respect everyone** - Not just those you perceive as having a higher status than yourself.

◆ **Respect differences in belief and opinion** - There will always be differences in culture, religious beliefs, political beliefs that should be handled in a courteous and civil manner. Respecting differences doesn't mean tolerating people who advocate harm to you or others.

◆ **Respect workspaces** - Any work area or space that you share with others should be treated with respect. Clean up after yourself.

◆ **Respect possession of others** - It is considered rude and inconsiderate to help yourself freely to anything that does not belong to you.

◆ **Communicating Respectfully** - Be a good listener. Practice listening more intently. Avoid negative body language with demeaning gestures. Avoid being condescending or patronizing.

◆ **Respectfully disagree** - You can respect someone's view even if you wholeheartedly disagree. The key is to disagree with what the person is saying without undermining the actual person's worthiness. No matter how hard you may try not to, you'll probably tread on someone's toes at some time or another. If the person is downright rude or mean, say your say and keep it moving without sinking to his or her level. My postal saying to disagreements while peering in the eye of the employee was: "That will be a negative"! Somehow that little phrase amongst us always served as an ice breaker towards a resolution.

◆ **Be respectful to others even if they're not respectful to you** - If the person is downright rude or mean - as difficult as it might be, try to show patience and humility. The other person just may actually learn something from you.

Leading with Honor

Honor is the key to all advancement -The world is filled with the pursuit of promotion. "Get Ahead" promises fill the bookshelves, with thousands of self-help manuals, leadership courses and business strategies to make it to the next level in the workplace.

There are authorities placed over you in life. You have to understand that even though they may not be believers, they are placed there by God. Give honor where honor is due.

The Bible says every person is subject according to the governing authorities. Whether Prime Minister or President of the United States, there is no one who has authority without God. We will later see that Daniel understood to succeed, he had to be subject to his governing authorities. Daniel understood when you submit to anyone in authority, you do not submit to man, you submit to God. When you can learn to honor authority, God can take you to a place of authority. But if you can't honor authority now, when you get to that position you covet, you will dishonor that position. The prep test for your promotion is how you honor those in authority now.

For there is no authority except from God, and those that exist have been instituted by God. Therefore, whoever resists the authorities resists what God has appointed, and those who resist will incur judgment. For rulers are not a terror to good conduct, but too bad. Would you have no fear of the one who is in authority? Then do what is good, and you will receive his approval, for he is God's servant for your good.

Romans 13:1-4

Do you comprehend the language of Honor?

"Authority must be honored whether leaders are just, kind, mean or provident. This speaks to you if you are in a leadership position or to you as one who's under authority. Our greatest example of honor is our Lord Jesus.

Luke 2:52 states that Jesus grew in wisdom and in stature and in favor with God and all the people.

Jesus learned how to honor his authorities. It wasn't enough to just honor His Father in heaven. He learned to honor the people appointed by God over his life, and thus, He grew in stature and favor before both.

Every environment requires the protocol of honor for a person to proceed. Every ministry, every new environment, even your marriage has a demon assigned to come to you and make you say and do things to lose favor and demote you from the place God has assigned. If we don't grow in character, not even prayer will help us enter the places where God wants to lift us. We may be disqualified from the promotion God wants to give if we do not learn honor in each environment!

Fair or not.... Honor!

No matter how anointed you are, you cannot dishonor your brothers. If you dishonor your brothers, you will lose the favor of your Father. Even if they are mean to you, you don't have the right to be mean in return. When you fight back, you become like them. The enemy's trick is to reduce you to their standard. Soon, you are no different than them and you lose the favor of God. Salt without flavor, is thrown into the refuse bin!

As Joseph became successful, an enemy came. The moment you purpose to honor, to learn the language of the house or whatever setting God has placed you in, you become a target of the enemy.

Don't breathe the air that dishonors what God is doing in your life. You cannot be part of that culture. Hear the tone. Walk away. You cannot entertain an environment of dishonor and expect to remain established. Even if one tries to arbitrate your language, the language of God must speak louder.

Simultaneously, when you are learning a new language, protect yourself so that you do not forget the language of God.

Learn to be in the world without letting the world come into you.

If you see that your language is getting corrupted, that should give you a sense of danger.

Refuse to be corrupted by the language you are learning. Be like Joseph, who refused Potiphar's wife, choosing prison over compromise, knowing the God whom he served. Jesus, when sending out his disciples, said "Be wise as serpents and innocent as doves." (Mathew 10:16). Be shrewd. Don't position yourself in a place where you can be compromised. Don't be overconfident. In your thinking, be shrewd, but in your actions, be like a dove. God is not responsible for the suffering you bring to yourself because you were not quick like the serpent. Joseph learned the language of prison so well; he was promoted to chief steward of the dungeon. If you don't learn the language of that greatness, it is only a matter of time that what was supposed to bless you, will kick you out. The faster you learn the language of honor specific to your setting, the faster you survive.

Two years later, when God delivered him, Joseph was promoted from slave to Prime Minster of Egypt in just one interview with the king.

Learn the language of honor in the house where God has placed you, so that you may thrive and advance in His glory!

THE CLASS OF LEADERSHIP – (Leadership Assessment V)
"GRACED" TO LEAD

As a Chaplain-Pastor, I believe the workplace is a mission field: a place to love the unlovable, a place to help and minister to the lost or to those who are soul-searching, a battlefield of divine assignment for Christians to experience, endure, and overcome for our good and development! Solid leadership has its foundation in God alone. This is something that the world does not follow. Godly leadership differs from worldly leadership. Christian leadership, Biblical leadership, is rooted in God. This means you put God above all other things-worldly success, worldly progression, and whatever else.

This level of assessment inquires of you, "How do you feel when you stand on the verge of reaching a long-awaited goal? Are you happy, sad, or relieved that the journey is nearly over? Are you frightened of the tests and trials that still lie ahead, or do you view your future with courage and faith in God?"

Joshua 1:6 "Be strong and of good courage: for unto this people shalt thou divide for an inheritance the land, which I swore unto their fathers to give them."

Notice God says, "…. for unto this people…" This is important because it reminds us that our leadership is connected to people!

When God calls you to accept a new assignment in life, it is going to require you to move into a new realm of faith, courage and boldness. You probably won't feel prepared for it, but God has counted you faithful enough to handle it, or the door would not have opened to you. You can do it!

In verse 6 of Joshua Chapter 1, God said, "Be strong and of good courage." In verse 7, He said, "Be strong and very courageous."

Then in verse 9, He said, "Have I not commanded thee? Be strong, and of good courage."

Joshua must have been thinking, "Why does God keep repeating these same words to me?" Because these are important elements of leadership. Be strong and courageous, doesn't mean you promote yourself so everybody will know how anointed you are. No. It means you use your strength to encourage and lead the people. A true leader is someone who is always using his strength to encourage and build up others. One who is always propping people up. There is a divine source of supply in him so strong that people draw courage and hope from him. Again, that's the reason for the statement "for unto this people." Your strength and courage are for the people! Strength and courage manifest encouragement!

◆ How you honor the person whom God places before you, is how you will enter your next level. People don't realize there are GATES in life. No matter how educated or rich you are life has a way of ensuring you can't go to certain places without going through a certain individual. A security guard may not have your degree, but he is certainly appointed by someone to guard the gate. Without submission to his authority, you will not pass through!

◆ Everybody tries to walk on glass when they first become the leader, because they want to be liked and they don't want to offend anybody. They want to be the friend of the people. There is no such thing if you are a leader. Not everybody is gonna like you or appreciate you or agree with you all the time. If you try to please everyone, you will please no one, and you certainly won't please God.

◆ If you fear the opinion of man, then the fear of man will dictate your decisions. If, on the other hand, you fear a holy God whom you know you will stand before one day, that fear of God will control and dictate your decisions.

◆ We spend most of our waking hours, it seems, on a job earning a living. That job overflows on us, for good or bad. Jobs can affect our relationship with God and ministry, with spouses, children, family, and friends. It can affect our outlook on people and society as a whole, good or bad, healthy or unhealthy.

◆ We're to be people who impact others positively and be unshaken and unmoved by the perilous and unstable things of this world. We as positive, impactful people leave a mark on peoples' lives. We leave a good impression, planting good seeds of life in the hearts and minds of men's souls and demonstrating God's love for all mankind.

◆ No matter what kind of gifts, titles, or anointing we have, it behooves us to be approachable people. When you present yourself friendly, approachable, reasonable, you will be surprised at the number of strangers and co-workers that will gravitate towards you in need with cases that need your prayers and Godly advice and direction. You could very well be the channel in which God uses to flow through.

◆ There will always be some who are closer to you than others. Affectionately named: **"The Sunshine Club"** was known as my inner circle. This group will most likely be an up close and personal testament of your character, your personality, the way you handle situations and react to all kinds of people. This is where flaws, imperfections, and unrealistic expectations of the leader are exposed and that to me is quite alright.

Moses, as the mighty prophet of God, was also a real human being with real imperfections. He had a strong personality. He wanted to completely control his ministry and do everything himself. Why is it do we feel "our way is the only right way"? or "if we want it done right, we feel as though we have to do it ourselves"? Ouch. I'm soooooo guilty!

The situation for Moses got so bad that his father-in-law, Jethro rebuked him and told him to start delegating authority to other people before it killed him. (Exodus 18:13-27).

I bring this point forth for two reasons:

Number (1): People always seem to have unrealistic expectations of anointed leadership. Because leaders are favored by God with a special grace, people somehow get the idea they are immune from normal living and human behavior. Because they are anointed, that somehow translates into they are exempt from carnality and fleshly reactions. We need to get a grip on this! People are people with flaws and imperfections. While we must respect the call of God upon them and recognize God promoted them into the position they hold, we must also allow them to function as normal human beings. Our human bodies are merely an "earthen vessel" but this does not minimize the "treasure" within.

Number (2): The demands we tend to put on ourselves as leaders tend to become unreasonable. Injustice is becoming the norm in most of our work world. You are on salary and are working 69 hours a week for 40 hours of pay and are still at risk of being disciplined, demoted, or fired. For many others, you are in an emotionally draining situation, caring for a family that includes young children and/or possibly elderly parents. Even though there is a huge drain on your physical and emotional reserves, you are the "call on" and "go to" person that feels overwhelmed in trying to bear up under the weight of being everybody's everything.

The weight of leadership is the sense of responsibility you carry that goes with your job. The problem is it never turns off easily. It follows you home. It accompanies you to bed. It travels with you to your medical appointments, to your child's basketball, softball practices, even on vacation. You can always leave work, but thanks to your phone, work never leaves you. It's hard to shake the weight of leadership. This is a description of me once upon a time and I had to be delivered! When the weight of leadership crushes you with its burdens, all of the benefits of feeling responsible for what you lead disappears. However, when it's appropriately governed, it can spur you toward leading better in a healthier way. Jesus promised that you don't need to do that. If you're truly leading in Him, you still bear a burden, but it's a light burden. (Matt 11:28)

MY EXPRESSION OF MARKETPLACE MINISTRY

I believe a level of uncertainty rest among many marketplace Christians of the spiritual gifts entrusted to them for fulfilling the Great Commission (Matt 28:19) in the teaching of all nations, preaching the Gospel in taking the saving message of Jesus Christ into all the world (Mark 16:15). Discipling and transforming lives extend world-wide as a part of our mission field. This is not limited to, but certainly includes marketplace

Christians being equipped to use their spiritual gifts in the marketplace where they spend most of their time. (Eph. 4:12).

Mission work not only takes place on the other side of the world. Our mission field is where we work, study, exercise, shop or wherever we may have some level of personal influence. Marketplace ministry involves exercising our spiritual gifts, the tools God has given to marketplace Christians for spreading the awareness of His light and glory throughout our workplaces and beyond. The business world is where the unbelievers are, where approximately 85 percent of Christians spend the majority of their waking hours, where evangelism and discipleship can happen on a daily basis and where the culture is shaped in transforming our communities and discipling nations.

Consider these opportunities for influence:
➢ the gift of faith in the workplace
➢ the gift of healing in the workplace
➢ the gift of worship in the workplace
➢ the gift of hospitality in the workplace
➢ the gift of compassion in the workplace ……. and of course, my very favorite

➤ A Business Leader i.e. USPS supervisor/manager with the gift of intercessory prayer in the workplace

Let's purposely and intentionally seek to graciously and generously extend the fruit of our labor as widely as possible to traverse the globe!!!

Social Skills – Joseph's service in prison was marked by the Lord's presence and thus we learn of his favor and fortune with Potiphar. Joseph's personal nature was basically trusting of people. In respect to people, he acquired the ability to create good relationships with others. He was extraordinary resourceful in dealing with people. He was a people's person. It was Theodore Roosevelt who said, "The most important single ingredient in the formula of success is knowing how to get along with people." Joseph mastered that skill.

Physical Appearance – Not only was Joseph handsome, he was also, physically fit. Now Joseph was handsome and well built.

Gen 39:6 – (MEV) So much so that Potiphar's wife became infatuated with him and tempted him to commit adultery with her.

We are mostly judged by appearances because it's the first thing visible seen. However, I believe we should not judge a book by its' cover. I realize that a few people in the world are not "beautifully challenged," but for the rest of us, we have to work at making ourselves presentable. You don't have to be a "bombshell" model or dress like a Hollywood star to be a leader;

but should always be appropriately well-groomed and neatly presentable for the occasion at hand.

Earned Trust - Joseph's integrity rejected the advances of Potiphar's wife. You build trust always with integrity and in an effort that shows genuine interest for personalized connections.

Second Timothy 3:17 says that scripture is given to equip the man of God for "all righteousness. "All righteousness includes things like marriage, being a good employee, and even being a great leader. The Bible is full of stories about leadership. I will continue exemplifying Godly character traits of leaders throughout the remaining chapters as I go deeper into unveiling hidden agendas of the culprit in the workplace and in our individual lives. Your character must be intact to sustain the pressure of spiritual warfare that inevitably comes.

Character Traits of Godly Leaders
Nehemiah is one of the most instructional books of the Bible as it relates to leadership.

The historical setting of the book of Nehemiah was during a crucial time known as postexilic period. This time period reflects the years after the return of the covenant people to their homeland after seventy years of captivity in Babylonia and Persia. There were three distinctive leaders that led these home-based journeys.

The first was led by Zerubbabel - a descendant of David who rebuilt the temple in Israel.

The second was led by Ezra - the priest who brought an initial spiritual revival in Israel.

The third return was led by Nehemiah, as told here. He began to rebuild both the walls and the spiritual lives of the people, and he became their governor.

God seeks to evolve leaders into maturity to help reconstruct, restore, and / or rebuild those things such as nations – tribes of people, communities of churches, systems, families, and individual lives that have deteriorated and broken down. The above-mentioned existence of entities has undoubtedly at specific points in time been diverted from the original intent of God.

Walls were very significant in ancient society as they served to provide protection from attacks of the enemy.

The building of the physical wall during Nehemiah's lifetime serves as a modern-day lesson for believers today. For example, the walls of salvation described in Isaiah 60:18 depicts the spiritual growth of a believer and it also represents the spiritual protection of God. Paul, in Ephesians 6 refers to our protection as the armor of God. Sadly, many have failed in the building up our spiritual wall of defense and remain unarmed as sitting ducks or open targets who are susceptible to the onslaughts of the adversary. The need therefore becomes apparent for the mature leaders walking in the spirit to arise and build according to God's original design. This is revealed in Galatians 6:1 which says "…. if another believer is overcome by some sin, you who are godly should gently and humbly help that person back onto the right path. And be careful not to fall into the same temptation yourself."

With Nehemiah, we see he was confronted and threatened on every hand by many fault-finding, critical disparagers because of his willingness to help Israel. Just because God has called you to do something great, does not necessarily mean smooth sailing for the task at hand. As a matter of fact, the more you yield to the plans and purposes of God, the more you're likely to come under enemy fire because you serve as a threat to the kingdom of darkness. Fret not beloved, this is normal spiritual protocol.

Nehemiah served as the personal cup bearer to the Persian king, Artaxerxes. He possessed great influence. He first showed his concern by asking questions of Hanani, his brother, who had just come from Judah.

Apathy, pride, lack of self-discipline Christ taught that awareness of sin was needed to do any type of effective ministry. In Matthew 7: 1-5 He taught that in order order to pluck the speck out of somebody else's eye, we must first take the log out of our own eye. Matthew 7: 1-5 he taught that.

Godly Leaders exemplifies Compassion and Concern

Christ expressed the virtues of compassion and concern towards the needs of people throughout his earthly ministry and so did Nehemiah after receiving distressing news about his native land. His broken heart motivated him for the task of restoring the temple walls and reconstructing the spiritual lives of his people.

Godly Leaders exemplifies Knowledge and Resourcefulness

John 6:12 points to the principle of resourcefulness demonstrated by Jesus. He said: "Gather up now the fragments (the broken pieces that are left over), so that nothing may be lost and wasted." Letting nothing be wasted definitely requires self-discipline in our age of consumerism.

Nehemiah enhanced his knowledge by objectively assessing the situation and its conditions to determine the cost beforehand. He then rallied resources by organizing a labor force to begin the building project.

Godly Leaders exemplifies a Lifestyle of Prayer Leaders guided by constant communication with God are spiritually sensitive in knowing: ...without Him we can do nothing. (John 15:5) We follow Jesus throughout the Scriptures as always slipping away into seclusion to pray. Jesus, Himself stated in John 8:28 "I do nothing of my own initiative"; and also in (John 5:19) He states: "....the Son is able to do nothing of Himself (of His own accord); but He is able to do only what He sees the Father doing, for whatever the Father does is what the Son does in the same way."

Nehemiah also prayed fervently before moving into action in approaching the king for permission to pursue the reconstruction project. Scriptures First Thessalonians 5:17 stating: Pray without ceasing; and Matthew 6:33 stating: Seek first the kingdom of God and his righteousness...–-concerning all things from the least miniscule to the most difficult dilemma are directives to live by accordingly. Such prayer warriors claim Gods' strength and guidance through prayer as they produce effective results of God's gift of Grace serving within their communities and sphere of influences.

Godly Leaders Exemplifies Humility and Transparency

Many leaders frequently notice the failures of others, but unfortunately, fail to see their own. They are judgmental and critical of the downfall and non-achievements of others. In turn, this affects how they are able to lead and reach others through ministry. Such leadership style mock that of the hypocritical Pharisees that practiced this double standard unbecoming conduct.

Godly leaders on the other hand are quick to identify the sin and shortcomings in their own lives through the posture of humility and the power of transparency. Check out Nehemiah's stance of humility prayed in Nehemiah 1:6. As he not only confessed the sins of the Israelites, but he included himself as well as his family.

Godly Leaders Protects Integrity Nehemiah's leadership contrasted with that of the selfish, corrupt "nobles and rulers." The corrupt leaders had selfishly abused their leadership role with the people. That was not the case with Nehemiah. (Nehemiah 5)

Godly Leaders Build Collaborative Teams

It was established that the wall of Jerusalem required extensive repairs. "And from that time forth, half of my servants worked at the task, and the other half held the spears, shields, bows, and coats of mail; and the leaders stood behind all the house of Judah (Nehemiah 4:16)." Teams of people jointly linked into the purpose or vision at hand will serve as a key component in finishing strong and successfully. Nehemiah overcame opposition with such dynamic, engaged teamwork.

Godly Leaders Acquire the skill to Wait on God

In today's society, leaders are known to be bold, with an over ambitious drive to pursue their goals in haste. Godly leaders characterize their waiting on God by discernment. Yes, there is a time to be active, but there is also a time to wait. Oftentimes, God sends you into a waiting period as He is preparing you for leadership. Waiting time is not wasting time. Certainly, we can see that though Nehemiah waited, he was not inactive. He spent day and night in prayer for months prior to the commencement of the task. (Neh 1:6).

Godly Leaders Persevere during Challenges

Nehemiah was personally attacked. He endured numerous trials, but he did not let that sway him. As the trials came, he stayed focused on the purpose at hand. He did not allow the obstacles to defeat him.

✓ Nehemiah 6:1-4 – They tried to get him to compromise
✓ Nehemiah 6:5-9 - They tried to slander him
✓ Nehemiah 6:10-19 - They tried to trick him
✓ Nehemiah 6:15-19 - They tried to threaten him

Joshua was also a humble servant who had great character.

Let us take a look at his character in Numbers 27:15-21. This passage occurs about the time Moses is going to die and he commissions Joshua to take over as leader. We never see Joshua seeking to climb a ladder of success or pursue a path in leadership. He served Moses because that was his assignment from God. That is what sustained him in hard times.

Today, people plan and scheme their way to the "top" and we applaud them for being hard workers, ambitious, industrious. We definitely want larger territories to serve Him, but we do not need to get ahead of Him to "make it happen". We all want the big assignment from God without heeding to our character. We must take ownership and be held accountable for the sustaining of our character. If we continually have to break down doors to serve, speak, write, lead, whatever we love doing in business or ministry, maybe we need to get on our knees and ask God to clarify our calling. Even with success, Joshua didn't ever have an inflated ego. And he always gave God the credit. Let's follow Joshua's loyalty as a follower and humility as a servant to pattern our own leadership character.

CHAPTER 3

CAREERS
WORKPLACE MENTORING

Prophetically Speaking,

God is moving on Millennials ....by way of A Spirit of Innovation! Though we can expect God to move on everyone, there is a special group that the Lord has begun to AWAKEN. Just as Jesus was 30 years old, so the Lord is awakening those who are in their 30s and considered millennials; and even younger. We are going to see those who have not been interested in the Lord suddenly awaken and find their purpose.

Millennials generally are described as those born in the 1980s and 1990s, which means the oldest members of the generation—also known as Generation Y—began entering the workforce in the late 1990s and early 2000s.

While most generations are connected to certain stereotypes and clichés, it's important to remember that employees still are individuals and should not be judged solely on the basis of when they were born. There are however some measurable differences in when and how millennials were raised and educated and understanding these differences can make it easier to connect with them in the workforce.

You may not realize it, but Abraham Lincoln, was raised poor and illiterate, was rebuffed by bankers, voters, employers, and law school deans before becoming President of the United States. Thomas Edison's teachers told him he was too dumb to learn anything – and he was fired from his first two jobs. Walt Disney was fired as a newspaper editor, with his boss saying he lacked imagination. Colonel Harland Sanders was told 1,009 times by restaurant owners before one who'd try his now famous fried chicken recipe. My point is this: Sometimes the biggest obstacles we face in life are the people around us, the people we need to convince to support us or the people of little vision who need us the most.

As a baby-boomer mother of two millennials, I found this resource as one of the most "on point" as it pertains to millennials.

A survey by Bentley University, showed 66% of Millennials had goals to start their own business. They want to succeed but understand the work-life balance they desire can often only be found by starting their own business. Millennials are the "customize-it" generation – from shopping online to video streaming. They want their user experience personalized to their preferences. Creating their career path is no different.

Bridging the generation gap within my sphere of influence, has afforded me the privilege in understanding that success is defined quite differently amongst generations. However, these could be viewed as age-related differences instead of generational differences. For us Baby Boomers, success is viewed as the prominent who's who bearing a title of honor. For Gen Xers, success is viewed as power of freedom to make one's own decisions. Millennials however view success as seizing windows of opportunity and capitalizing on favorable circumstances presented to gain influence and make an overall impact. More Independence and even more so-flexibility.

The aspect of flexibility is another main driver for these young minded entrepreneurs. Although it is popularly believed that Millennials have an entitlement complex and regretfully withdrawals from hard work, it is of my opinion this to be a preconceived notion of faulty facts rather than verifiable truths. My work experience with Millennials accredits their flexibility towards work hours for the allowance of a larger playing field in maximizing their potential. Thus, this serves most beneficial in their ability to thrive, and flourish while developing and producing more favorable and profitable results. The concurrent concept of converting inputs into more useful outputs is achievable largely due to their proficiency in technology that has been engrafted within the nature of this special tribe.

The Elite Class of Baby Boomers
The greatest act of a leader is MENTORING!

Mentoring provides a great opportunity to utilize us baby boomers, but only when companies recognize that mentoring is a significant piece of a strategic plan to ramp up recruiting, retaining and increasing the knowledge and skills of talented employees.

Having a heart for this generation as a chaplain-pastor, and mentor - this subject matter is quite dear to me. I believe no matter how anointed we are, we have to be conscious of the language of the generation around us.

In obedience to the Lord and as one of my Kingdom assignments in the earth, I host an on-demand event: "A Divine Call of A Divine Exchange" comprised of young men and women partially my spiritual sons and daughters whom the Lord has impressed upon me to "Add Value" to their lives by imparting truth and wisdom through messages of Hope and Grace.

In the Word of God (2 Kings 13:21), it says that the Moabites were burying a man and they put him in the tomb of

Elisha, and when the man's body touched the bones of Elisha – the man was revived and stood on his feet. Now when we hear that – a lot of us rejoice because the anointing of God was so strong in the ministry of Elisha that it soaked into his very bones and it was powerful enough to actually raise the dead to life.

Yet, the other thing about this passage of scripture to recognize is this: The anointing on Elisha life was not passed to the next generation, but instead it died with him. I believe the anointing was supposed to continue on but in order for the transfer of anointing to be complete, a spiritual son/daughter or mentee must be postured to receive what is given. It may well be that Elisha would have transferred the anointing, but the sad thing is, there was no one able to receive it....

An established business, company, or ministry will fade away and become ineffective if there is no one to carry it on.

As a mentoring baby boomer and mother of millennials, I've learned the effectiveness of mentoring must be done strategically and creatively. Mentoring the whole person is a key component. In this segment we will highlight mentoring in the light of professionalism and spirituality. The development of the whole person entails achieving a balanced lifestyle. There must be balance.

It is factual that Millennials now make up the largest part of the workforce. My interrelationship and social involvement with this unique generation has enlightened me thoroughly in highlighting the following attributes of Millennials:

✓ Millennials are Innovative

✓ Millennials are Impactful

✓ Millennials are naturally entrepreneurial

✓ Millennials value experiences

✓ Millennials are redefining success

✓ Millennials currently dominate the workforce

✓ Millennials prefer working in a flexible environment

✓ Millennials are frequently over-qualified

✓ Millennials are charitable and most generous

✓ Millennials are financially-savvy

✓ Millennials are multi-taskers

✓ Millennials are diverse

✓ Millennials are a huge demographic

✓ Millennials are virtually connected via social media

✓ Millennials expend excessive time on their smart phones

✓ Millennials desire to make a difference

✓ Millennials loves traveling

✓ Millennials loves their dogs

✓ Millennials are fearless risk-takers

✓ Millennials are less religious

✓ Millennials value family and friends

✓ Millennials prefer career before marriage

Upon the rude awakening of younger employees experiencing dissatisfaction with their companies, they tend to voice a frustrating sound describing the difficult and over-whelming demands placed upon them by their bosses in the workplace. The intentions of these bosses however may very well be for moral good but lack sensitivity in its approach. I have found it is paramount to attentively hear out these inexperienced employees on the subject matter and to address their concerns offering solutions that have yielded past favorable results. Businesses abroad should seek to gain the benefits of utilizing experienced, multifaceted Baby Boomers as mentors or consultants to help channel these high stress levels of frustrations appropriately; and provide guidance and encouragement along the path to fulfillment.

Provide fresh perspectives - Today, jobs are about more than just upward mobility. As a matter of fact, this generation of Millennials are redefining success and no longer climbing the traditional ladder of success just to later learn the ladder is leaning against the wrong wall. The commodity of time must not be squandered; and thus, the vast experience of mentors sharing their do's and don'ts will help to minimize friction or bypass the ditches and glitches altogether.

Build skills - Mentoring can also help mature employees learn from and understand other generations. For instance, younger employees can help baby boomers with technical skills or provide marketing insights about a new community of buyers.

Reduce generational conflict - The most common generational conflicts that I've arbitrated in resolving are those relating to differences in expectations of work policies and regulations; particularly addressing conduct and behavior issues, proper dress codes, the scheduling of reporting times, and the infamous cell phone usage while performing work duties. I recall having to intervene in applying the wisdom of a millennial mother's experience to diffuse many heated conflicts throughout my tenure as supervisor.

These are some typical examples of younger employees questioning management in a brazen manner:

"Why can't we work early hours like everybody else?" "Why do we have to work every Sunday?"

"What about my childcare issues?" Mentors can often manage, explain and process this information better than most upper-level managers who are out of touch with the day-to-day operations. My personal involvement and intervention most often proved effective because of the rapport established through relationship.

Distribute the wealth transfer. Baby boomers possess the experience to distribute a wealth of knowledge. Sadly, they all too often depart ways into the next unfolding chapter of their life, taking with them vast volumes of resources without sharing such knowledge of power.

Recognize and Reward Mentoring. Now faced with large numbers of employees getting ready to retire and the need to on board younger workers, and quickly move them up to supervisory and managerial positions; Mentors can help these new supervisors and managers develop a business-related understanding and strategize about using the talents of more experienced employees.

A good way to attract baby boomers to become workplace mentors is to provide incentives for their contributions is to hype up mentoring in the board rooms, at the contract negotiating tables and most important – Give honor to whom honor is due by including them in recognition/award programs.

Continue Consulting & Maintain Mentoring past retirement - Many of my counterparts (baby boomers) and I have considered working past the traditional retirement age in managing our multiple streams of income. This ability and willingness to create momentum beyond mediocrity speaks volume in being rated as an aspiring achiever committed to results. Oh, what honor of sustainable impact in creating lasting legacies!

Let's conclude this chapter by... Imparting Wisdom

Wisdom is usually confused with knowledge, but there's a big difference. Knowledge involves the accumulation of facts. Wisdom is the ability to apply the knowledge to achieve the best outcome. The wisdom of God equips and prepares you for God's purposes. It strengthens you in the certainty of your salvation so you can overcome confusion, falsehood, and uncertainty with the

God-given confidence that comes through Christ alone. Wisdom comes from living and learning, from a hunger to learn and grow throughout a lifetime. The more you humble yourself and keep a hungry heart, the more wisdom you'll acquire.

CHAPTER 4
MY SECRET PLACE
AT THE FEET OF JESUS

MANTLED FOR PRAYER

Prayer is Foundational in the Life of an Overcomer

"Pray without ceasing" (I Thessalonians 5:17).

Jesus said it this way: "Men always ought to pray and not lose heart" (Luke 18:1).

The MSG Bible says: Prayer is essential in this ongoing warfare.

Prayer is foundational for me as it is also my lifestyle.

Prayer serves as a life-birther in the sense that it gives birth.

Prayer is essential to making your vision or goal happen. Not only is it the way you are going to know the specific boundaries and perimeters of your vision but is the only way you can find out how, when, where, and with whom you are to proceed.

Just praying in general terms is not enough – you've got to ask the Holy Spirit for a specific strategy, and then begin to do what He tells you to do. If all you do is work a plan that seems right or that your organization or denomination has always used, then you are not operating from a spiritual foundation and you have no support for what you are trying to achieve. You've got to build a foundation to sustain your vision or goal, and prayer will build that foundation.

There are many good resources for learning how to pray, but as I tell my students of Prayer – the best way to learn how to pray is to pray. Pray in the ways that come naturally, then grow and mature your practice of prayer steadily.

Pray like the success of the whole project depends completely on God but work like the success of the whole project depends completely on you! This powerful combination of prayer and hard work always produces marvelous fruit in the kingdom of God. If you're in the business world and desire to move further ahead in your company or profession, how are you going to do it? Sitting at your desk or at the park on lunch break simply wishing about your future will not accomplish anything.

You start out by praying in faith asking the Holy Spirit to impart a plan, an idea, an objective, a strategy to get you from where you are to where you want to be. That new assignment at your company or workplace will not come to you by itself. You must take the necessary steps in moving toward your goal.

Our goal as OVERCOMERS is to be able to reach out in prayer at any moment and immediately be in touch with God.

Our whole life can be prayer as we walk day by day with Him. Don't sweat the details, leave those to God. Just pray!

The frequent most asked questions from my students are:

1) If God is all - powerful and all-knowing, why do we need to pray?

2) Why doesn't God do for us what He knows needs to be done?

3) What power drives our prayer?

God does not move on the earth, unless His covenant people pray. "Well, hasn't He already done it?" "Yes, it's already done." It's a finished work, but it's not manifesting on you or in your life without your consent. Prayer serves as your consent!

Hebrews 5:7 tells us that Jesus prayed for what He needed. It is the Holy Spirit who lives within us that fuels our prayers. He determines the character and the content of our prayers. He knows your heart, and He knows the Father's heart, because He is one with the Father. Therefore, He knows your intent when you pray. He takes your fumbling prayers and reshapes them to reveal the deepest needs beneath the surface of your words.

Over the past 30 years, I have gone through several iterations of prayer and continue progressing from glory to glory in my prayer life. One thing I've purposed never to let go of and that is self-examination.

Two of my most favorite everyday prayers for soul searching is Psalm 139:23-24 and Malachi 3:3.

Search me Oh God, know my heart: try me and know my thoughts: And see if there be any wicked way in me and lead me in the way everlasting.

Sit on the throne of my heart as a refiner and a purifier. I give you the purging consent. Purify me Oh Lord!

Self-Examination most often requires you to ask yourself:

"What is my problem?" "What is the root of my stinky attitude?" And don't automatically look around and point the finger. "It's her, It's him, It's my boss, it's them over there." This is not a prayer to pray if you don't wanna know the truth. I assure you if you dare to take the stance for God to shine His spotlight on you, He absolutely will and reveal You to You!

Wait until you later read of the astounding truth revealed to me one morning during prayer. It was breath-taking. The most shocking thing I had heard during prayer!!!

If you have any doubts about the importance of prayer, please consider its high place in the life and ministry of our

Lord. I recall once reading this impressionable version of one's prayer life.... It was not only His regular habit, but His resort in every emergency, however slight or serious. When perplexed He prayed. When hard pressed by work He prayed. When hungry for fellowship, He found it in prayer. He chose His associates and received his messages upon His knees. If criticized, he prayed. If fatigued in body or wearied in spirit, He had recourse to his one unfailing habit of prayer. There was no emergency, no difficulty, no necessity, no temptation that would not yield to prayer.... WOW! How much prayer meant to Jesus!

If the Lord Jesus considers it important for Him to pray, and He has been interceding for us at the throne of God for the last two thousand years, maybe those of us who are less than diligent in our prayer life should stop and examine ourselves.

As one woman prayed, "Dear Father in heaven, so far today I've done pretty well. I haven't gossiped or lost my temper; I haven't been greedy, grumpy, nasty, selfish, or overindulgent. But, God in a moment I'm going to get out of bed. And from that point on, I'm going to need a lot of help from you."

To be up and awake means the battle is engaged. As an overcomer, the enemy will attack you with distractions, doubts, and temptations to abandon prayer. Guard your prayer time and keep your prayers constantly flowing. Prioritize prayer as you plan your schedules. Desire spiritual maturity. This is how you fight the fight of faith in keeping a good attitude. Learn to be thankful and intentionally grateful. You can achieve this because in your soul, there's a deeper part of us that can activate our faith and that's our spirit man, and with our spirit, we can fight all the nonsense of the carnal man that comes against our soul and we thus, win as OVERCOMERS. You must be a fighter in the right fight in life.

You may not feel "ready" for your next new assignment from God, but that's alright. God knows you're ready and He will provide the grace and power in equipping you to readiness. Suddenly and supernaturally, the Holy Spirit joins with you in the rhythm of prayer. In all of His wonderful attributes and personality, He feels everything you feel. He understands the complete inadequacy that you experience. He understands the battles that you are facing. He willingly falls into that circumstance with you, feeling each motion and frustration. Then He begins a plan of rescue. The word intercession means "to fall in with someone else."

MARKED FOR INTERCESSION

Prayer is jurisdictional and enforces the judgment and justice of Heaven in situations.

Love, honor, respect, humility and purity are the core values of the kingdom entrusted in the forming of my prayer life as a prophetic intercessor.

As the crucifixion of **"self"** took place in my life - intercession begun. Whereas I began sensing the burden of the Lord to pray not only for my four and no more; but for others, situations, nations, government and other spheres of society. What a privilege to be counted worthy to participate with the Lord in subduing the enemy and releasing God's creation into its' destiny through prophetic prayer and intercession. Intercession takes mental strength and spiritual fortitude.

Intercessors have influence in the spirit. Intercessors have a powerful God-given grace to shift atmospheres and cultures through their prayers. Intercessors open gateways to God's presence that permeate every priority in their social culture.

The Sword that Pierced my Soul

As we are impending upon spiritual warfare in the up- coming chapters, I thought it would be fitting to use this segment of intercession as a bridge to cross over into spiritual warfare. From an intercessor's perspective... "the initial level of warfare always begins with you.

Bear in mind my two favorite everyday soul-searching prayers as you read this segment.

As an intercessor, in 2007, one of my very first spiritual warfare assignments were administered through my church ministry. Without going into specific details just know that this was a very weighty warfare assignment that had attracted what I call the "hit and run tag team twins." Intercessors beware of these Siamese twins, **the Binding Spirits of backlash and retaliation.**

It's important to continue in your attitude of worship, prayer and warfare after a glorious victory; because this is the time that most people tend to want to relax and go to sleep. These petty demons full of resentment and fury are known to get angry and attack immediately after spiritual victories. They return loaded with vengeance.

Their blow can be detrimental and knock you off your feet if you are not prepared or aware. They seldom attack when you are spiritually conscious. They wait till you are vulnerable - after you've left the church service, after a mighty move of God, after you've just received a prophetic word, or after you've sown seeds, before launching their attacks.

The suffering of backlash and retaliation was the brunt of the church hurt I experienced a few months after the assignment. However, I was obligated to remain on my post throughout the persecution until the release came. I left the ministry in 2008. As I was waiting and seeking God for direction, I would periodically become engaged with conversations as to the details of what occurred and the reason for my leaving the ministry. But even more so, I began replaying the unfolding situation over in my thoughts - all the intricate details of everything that had taken place. This is a short version of my "venting session" unto the Lord.

"Lord, help me to understand the underlining of why certain attacks occurred after the warfare assignment. You planted me in this ministry as an intercessor. Trained me to bring every matter before Heaven and not men (especially those I didn't quite understand). And that I've done. I've only tried to do what you've told me to do (hear and obey). Nobody but You know the sacrifice I've made for this ministry; the nights of fasting, praying, and sleeplessness. And I did it in love without ever complaining. Even praying for the very ones who I know are against me. And now, the leader whom You assigned me to cover secretly in prayer is now speaking curses against me. What betrayal! Really God? Is this my reward?"

Once upon a time I was surprised; but no longer, as my contending for the faith has been with professing Christians (the wolves who pervert the faith).

As many tears as it may have cost Paul, virtually all his letters have to do with contentions that he was having with professed Christians. (Phil 3:18)

Prayer is an indispensable part of contending for the faith. "Praying in the Holy Spirit." Unless we seek the mind of the Holy Spirit in prayer, we will not grow in our grasp of the faith and we will be weak contenders.

On the morning of March 7, 2008, I got up to pray and as usual I began seeking what the Lord was requiring of me for this day at hand. Was it praise? Was it worship? Was it travail? Was it interceding for a particular person or situation? Or was it just to sit quietly in His presence and meditate on the Word. Well, I quickly learned that it wasn't any of those things. Instead, it was warfare! Enforcing the enemy's defeat was something I had become versed in. Charged and excited in my spirit man I quickly pulled out my sword, ready to do battle. I began asking the Lord to expose the enemy. "Which strongman? What demonic stronghold? Where was the culprit hiding?" I was geared up in my spirit to go at it and enforce the victory! And then I heard the ever so shocking words: "Use the Sword on You!!!" "What?" I said, as though the Lord stuttered. "Use the Sword on You!!!" I dropped to my knees. Everything came to a screeching halt. "Oh my God, but what is this? And why?" He said to me, "You see, as so often as you replayed the hurt in your mind, and began rehearsing all of the assignments you accomplished - I used those things to be a time of self-reflection; causing you to see every toxic thing had begun to breed in your heart; false humility, offense, betrayal unforgiveness, and pride. Although you didn't outwardly brag about the situation – still those things were festering in your heart as I began to search you out. You see, you were so quick to tell me of your faithfulness in all of your right doings, and now you too have been found guilty in failing the heart test. Now, bring the sword to the altar and use it on yourself. If you confess and repent, I will forgive and restore.

Every day, I laid on the altar. I went through a spiritual death process until the Lord cleansed and restored me completely. You see, those controlled by the flesh cannot please God and a prideful, haughty, unforgiving spirit does not bring Glory to God.

The Word of the Lord declares: *Do not lift up your horn on high: do not speak with a stiff neck (Psalm 75:5)*; and that is exactly what I was found guilty of.

Lord knows, I learned my lesson. After that experience, I didn't ever wanna hear or even see that cutting angle of the "sword" ever again!!!

I eventually saw where that attitude not only limited my influence but had increased spiritual warfare. I was playing into the enemy's hands. Until I repented of my selfish ambition, I was giving room for that snake to operate through my prayer life. Once I decided to humble myself and gave up my right of entitlement to be acknowledged, the atmosphere in me and around me quickly changed. Our character must be found intact.

This Word is meant to empower intercessors to know the true power and influence we have in the spirit. Determine always to guard your heart so that your intercession is a sweet-smelling incense before the Lord that tips the bowls of heaven, bringing revival and transformation to your environment.

CHAPTER 5

SPIRITUAL WARFARE

EXPOSING THE CULPRIT

Through much prayer, studying the Word of God and biblical-based articles, I've compiled this segment to pull back the curtain and expose evil personality traits of the most glaringly obvious wicked culprits hiding in the workplace. Particularly, greed, jealousy, and the Jezebel spirit are amongst those in which I've battled against face to face and in hand to hand combat.

Spiritual Warfare is done by the spirit and the battleground of this psychological warfare is the mind. Thus, it has to do with taking authority over your mind and your flesh, as well as taking authority over the works of darkness. This same war is fought on every level of humanity. It is fought in the family, on school grounds, in corporate headquarters, and even in nations. Regardless of your social status, workspace, work environment, believer or unbeliever, we are ALL subject to a level of warfare in our daily regimen. Oftentimes, we will have to confront to conquer to reclaim territory.

Self is a snare on the battlefield. The soul is the seat of our emotions, our personality; the soul is the essence of who we really are. Subsequently, the more you feed your soul spiritual things, the more spiritual you will become. On the other hand, the more you feed your soul carnal things, the more carnal you become as a person.

Many verses in the Bible refer to our "enemies." We may have a tendency to think of only human enemies. But our real enemies are not human at all. Remember that our battle is not against flesh and blood. When you read the word "enemies" in the relating verses of this segment, think of Satan and his demons.

The phrase spiritual warfare can be a bit intimidating and frightening to some; especially newly believers, disciples or new converts. I accepted Jesus as my personal Savior at the age of 16. I was glad to know Jesus and thanked God for saving me. I wanted to learn to love him more and not worry about all that warfare stuff.

I remember thinking as a young lady "Oh, I'm not gonna need that part of my Christianity." I figured if I just be good, do good, learn how to mind my own business I wouldn't need to know anything about warfare. The thought that there was an enemy that wanted to destroy me was intimidating because I had not yet come into the knowledge and truth of what the Word of God says about it. Oh, how immature that type of thinking was! The believer's warfare is different from those who are not born-again believers. We cannot allow them to instruct us on how to fight.

When we think of spiritual warfare we cannot think of God versus Satan as an equal battle. It's not an equal fight. God is Greater. Satan is not God nor is he a god. He is a being created by God. God is greater and greater is He that is in us than he that is in the world.

Too many Christians are deceived to the point they do not believe in the power of Satan and the awful influence of the demonic. There is indeed an active plot against our families and every one of us individually. Most of the time, we are ignorant of the war raging around us. Beloved, ignoring the truth leads to disaster. In 2 Corinthians 2:11, we are warned: "not to be ignorant of Satan's devices."

THE CHARACTER OF THE ENEMY

•Satan is a real enemy

Some various titles given to indicate his personality: liar, thief, murderer, deceiver, accuser, tempter, prince, etc. Scripture references: Job 1: 6; Isaiah 14:12; Matthew 4:10; 9:34; 10:25; John 8:44 and 12:31; 2 Corinthians 2:11; 1 Thessalonians 2:18 and 3:5; and 2 Thessalonians 2:9-11.

• Satan occupies an exalted position

He has a "kingdom" (Matthew 12: 26); he is "the god of this age" (2 Corinthians 4:4) He is the prince of this world" (John 12:31; 14:30; 16:11), showing his dominating influence the lives of "those who are disobedient" (Ephesians 2:2). He is "the prince of the power of the air" (Ephesians 2:2), indicating his control over evil spirits and he is an imposter of true Christianity (2 Corinthians 11:14; and 1 Timothy 4: 1)

Although Satan retained his intelligence and power after the Fall, his power never did and never can exceed the power of Almighty God. Satan may have knowledge, but he is the greatest fool of all. No matter how powerful Satan may seem, he is under divine control and cannot do anything outside of God's permissive will. Satan may have caused the fall, but he is not all-powerful. As we engage in spiritual warfare, we must always remember that Satan is already defeated!

However, although defeated, he can tempt us, mislead us, and even influence us in making us believe that we are separated from God. This is his tool in diminishing our effectiveness in fulfilling our Kingdom assignments.

Satan's strategy is to wage war by using psychological warfare and overwhelming force. This is war!

His strategy is applied through 3 basic means: intimidation, manipulation and domination. The trappings are different, but domination and manipulative control are still the undercurrent. There are 3 temptations to sin that everyone experiences: lust of the flesh, lust of the eye, and the pride of life (1 John 2:16) Needless to say, every sin we commit will be preceded by at least one of these temptations.

Satan tempted Jesus in the wilderness to stray from the Father's plan. He set before the Lord the lust of the flesh, the lust of the eye, and the pride of life. He tempted Jesus' body, soul and spirit. We should make no mistake about what the clear purpose of Jesus was in coming into the world. He came to do battle with Satan. For this reason, was the Son of God made manifest – that He would destroy the works of the devil. (I John 3:8)

Just because it sounds good, feels good, and tastes good doesn't mean it's right. Just because everybody else is doing it doesn't mean you should. It is very easy to succumb to the ways of the world, to compromise our standards until our lives are characterized by the lusts of the flesh. As Christians, however, we are called to a higher standard.

What is lust of the flesh? Those things that satisfy our natural man but defiles our spirit man. Galatians 5:19-21 provides several examples of lustful behavior.

All demonic spirits are "flesh feeders"--they gain their foothold and their strength by feeding on our carnal nature (flesh).

- Demons are under the authority of believers and can only affect us if we give them the space to do so.
- Demons cannot enter you without legal ground and you do not have to tolerate them.
- Demons enter through open doors, which means they have to be given an opportunity.

In other words, you just don't pick up a demon by walking down the street and accidentally bumping into one that's looking for a home. No, they enter thru the gateways and doors of sins (sins of omission and commission)

A GATEWAY – *is a place of authority where dominion is exercised and whoever controls* your life's different gateways exercises authority, dominion and control over you. Whoever gains control of your mind will eventually gain control of your life.

When we engage the enemy on the level of personal deliverance, we are fighting Satan's front-line troops. The first objective in warfare is to free oneself. While we have walked in ignorance and darkness the enemy has successfully made inroads into each of us. We must learn how to get him out and how to keep him out.

Our Enemy is Defeated, but still Dangerous

Strongman that he is, he has been dispossessed by one STRONGER. Therefore, as long as we stand firm in Christ, we will be able to have victory over all Satan's attacks. So, stand your ground. After Jesus, he shares this parable, "When a strong man, fully armed guards his own palace, his goods are safe; but when one stronger than he attacks him and overcomes him, he takes away his armor in which he trusted and divides his spoils (Luke 11: 21-22 ESV)." In this story, Satan is the strong man and Jesus is the Stronger One who overtakes him. Even more, Jesus has disarmed Satan. This truth is confirmed in Colossians 2:15 which tells us that Jesus disarmed the rulers and authorities and put them to open shame by triumphing over them in Him. Colossians 2:10 also reminds us that it doesn't matter how many powers of darkness and principalities there are, all authority is Christ's. You also are complete through your union with Christ who is the head over every ruler and authority. (Colossians 2:10 NLT).

STRONGHOLD(S)

Stronghold – can be defined in both the natural (physical) and spiritual realms. Naturally, strongholds are used by the military as for protection. Spiritually, the word is translated from a Greek word that means fortress; something or some part of our life that Satan has surrounded. They are hiding places for demonic and unclean spirits in a person's life. They hide in crevices. Strongholds begin in the mind. Therefore, the biggest battle is in the mind and in our thinking. If we allow those thoughts to continue unchecked, they become a sinful behavior, which then becomes more difficult to overcome. And if we're not careful, just like that, we've given place to the devil through a sin that worked its way through our lives.

Strongholds can't be reason away. They will not go away over time – they only get worse. Strongholds must be broken down, torn down, demolished; remember they are like a fortress. The stronghold in your life not only endangers you – but it endangers your family and others around you.

Before proceeding, let's establish this truth, "Do these strongholds only afflict the unbeliever who has not accepted Christ? Are they only the problem of the unbelieving world and not the concern of the Christian?" Absolutely not! Strongholds are dungeons of captivity running rampant in the minds of Christians and greatly hindering our walk with God and our Christian growth. Deception is the glue that holds every stronghold together.

STRONGHOLDS – The devil builds a fortress in a place in our lives that we have given over to him that should be occupied by the Spirit of God!

STRONGHOLDS - Represent a place in our minds and hearts where the enemy has become entrenched and where we have become in bondage to Satan.

STRONGHOLDS – A point of operation where Satan can keep a person captivated, incapacitated, and under control. It is an emotional, mental or experiential mind-set that thrusts the heart into bondage and keeps it from growing spiritually in the Lord. It's a mental fortress of wrong thinking.

STRONGHOLDS – Feed off sin; and the fences grow higher, thicker and more twisted the more sin dominates our thinking.

STRONGHOLDS – The only way strongholds can be destroyed is through the power of God. They are removed from your mind and heart in degrees by removing the layers with your cooperation and obedience. The dark kingdom is driven out little by little because spiritual warfare, like every day real warfare is ongoing.

Depression, anger, rejection, negative thinking, gossip, lying, bitterness, unforgiveness, greed, covetousness, hypocrisy is to name a few common strongholds.

Fear is a huge stronghold and it's the foundation of many other strongholds. Fear itself is a natural response to a threat. We would be foolish not to have some fear and respect for danger, whether it be natural or man-made. But to be controlled by fear, when fear is used as a deliberate tool of the enemy, is a different matter entirely. It has many servants, such as fear of failure, fear of authority, and fear of intimacy. Doubt and unbelief are distrusting spirits of fear. Its primary purpose is to keep us incapacitated so we will not draw near to God and begin to operate our lives by faith.

Fear of Man

Is there someone in your life who causes fear to rise in your spirit? The fear of man brings a snare, but whoever trust in the Lord shall be safe. The fear of man is something that really grips our young people today. Peer pressure, the fear of being different, the fear of what other people will think can take over our lives. I'm not advocating obnoxious, but here's the truth: it doesn't matter what anybody thinks but God! Young people and adults alike need to quit allowing the fear of man to hinder what God wants to do in our lives and just develop an attitude to be the best version of you.

Fear of Insignificance

Fear was the case of Israel when God led them to the front porch of the Promised Land. The faithless majority of the spies saw the obstacles and took their eyes off God, focusing instead on giants and grasshoppers. They looked at their own ability saying, "We are not able" (Numbers 13:31) and they were right. They were not able in their own strength to overcome the inhabitants of the land. They had to change their perception to see God's abundance as a devouring beast before which they were helpless.

Whenever we are poised to enter some new and greater dimension of God, the enemy will use fear to stop us in our tracks.

Fear of the Future

When you engage the spirit of fear, he brings along his tormenting buddies. Fear never comes alone. Fear's best friend is torment. Fear and torment gain access into your life through wrong relationships. The enemy sees the power and purpose that God is bringing us into, so he plants a minefield of fear on the frontier of our inheritance (that which the Lord has predestined for our lives).

Overcoming Fear

The apostle John gave the answer when he wrote:

Perfect love cast out fear (I John 4:18)

For God has not given us a spirit of fear, but of power and of love and of a sound mind" (2 Timothy 1:7)

Bitterness

Bitterness spreads quickly from one person to the next; just as a small spark in the woods can kindle a forest fire. Bitterness defiles the entire body. A little bitterness can poison and weaken an entire workforce. Bitterness stemming from jealousy and pride prevents us from hearing the ways to improve our lives, businesses and ministries.

Overcoming Bitterness

To walk in freedom, we must put away wrong words as instructed in Ephesians 4:31: **"Let all bitterness, wrath, anger, clamor, and evil speaking be put away from you, with all malice."** Also, we must show forgiveness and pardon others. I like the word pardon because when one is pardoned, his or her crime is no longer subject to further inquiry, scrutiny, discussion, or explanation. If someone is pardoned from a prison sentence, he or she was once in jail and now is out of jail. It's that simple. In today's language, we allow others "off the hook." Ephesians 4:32 says it this way: **"And be kind to one another, tenderhearted, forgiving one another, just as God in Christ forgave you."** Finally, we must pursue peace. The word peace means that everyone in a society or relationship operates harmoniously. Notice that it doesn't mean we operate the same. We celebrate our godly differences in our common pursuit of righteousness.

Pursue peace with all people, and holiness, without no one will see the Lord: looking diligently lest anyone fall short of the grace of God: lest any root of bitterness springing up cause trouble, and by this many become defiled". (Hebrews 12:14-15)

This means we do not allow bad talk, unforgiveness, or poison to take root in our lives.

Forgiveness is just as important as warring against demonic forces, because it destroys the "gate", or point of access the enemy uses to gain a foothold (stronghold) in the victim's life. The past must be put behind to allow the Lord to heal us. Forgive the person (ourselves included) involved and forgive God.

Rejection

This is the point of access most frequently used by the enemy for establishing a demonic stronghold. In order to gain influence, or to strengthen its influence upon us, the spirit of rejection distorts everything that occurs in our lives into feelings of acceptance or rejection, to keep our focus on ourselves, instead of turning to God for the love we need. It opens the door to many other spirits to gain controlling access to our souls. Paranoia and self-pity are common servants of rejection and are usually present to some degree.

Overcoming Rejection

Jesus gives us the ultimate example of how to thrive through rejection. From the onset of His ministry, He encountered opposition, disbelief, rejection *(Luke 4:16-29)*. People questioned his authority and authenticity *(Mark 6:3, John 5:43; 6:64-67)*. He even told his disciples to expect rejection by the world (John 15:18).

Do not allow your identity to be defined by how others view you. Our identity must also be independent from any work we do. Instead we must focus on the truth of who we are, and the truth is that through Christ, you are chosen, redeemed, and created for good works. As Christ's ambassadors, we must follow his example which requires us to stay resolute to what we know to be true about who we are in Christ. *(Luke 9:51-56; Eph 2:8-10)*

HOW TO MANAGE STRONGHOLDS

James 4:7 says "Submit yourselves therefore to God. Resist the devil, and he will flee from you". When submitted to God, we have authority over the devil. You must first then be SUBMITTED; because if not, the enemy will not be thwarted at all. Why? Because your unwillingness to submit to God continues giving the enemy a foothold. After recognizing the stronghold in your life, sin must be purged, and a life of commitment must be continued.

Confession. When you confess, you're saying, "Ok God, I come into agreement with that which you are showing me about me," and it means you are then condemning and renouncing it before the Lord. He then judges it and whatever strongman or demonic stronghold is in operation against you, is bought in the light by your obedience in **confessing, repenting,** and **renouncing** it. This armor of light is needed to breakdown the veil of darkness surrounding us. Henceforth, the stronghold is then destroyed by the power of God.

WEAPONIZED FOR WAR

2 Corinthians 10:3, *For though we walk in the flesh, we do not war after the flesh.*

No psychological counseling, no self-help book or life class can completely annihilate these strongholds without Christ. The weapons of the flesh lack the spiritual power to blow these strongholds out of our minds and hearts. These fortresses can only be obliterated by spiritual weapons rooted in Jesus Christ. Only God's mighty weapons disassembles and decimate every brick of the strongholds that captivate our hearts.

For the weapons of our warfare are not carnal, but mighty through God to the pulling down of strong holds;) Casting down imaginations [or intents], [or arguments] and every high thing that exalts itself against the knowledge of God and bringing into captivity every thought to the obedience of Christ. And having in a readiness to revenge all disobedience, when your obedience is fulfilled (2 Corinthians 10:4-6).

These arguments are expressed in a variety of ways, including criticism, gossip, innuendo, sarcasm, moodiness and religious pretense, as well as others.

Satan's fortress will crumble before us if we wield our weapons. When you cast away these strongholds, every demon that has lurked behind these lies, habits, sicknesses, and wrong choices is exposed, and God punishes their disobedience. When we are full of obedience, then God will take revenge on every demon that has dared to threaten you.

Put on the Whole Armor

THE ARMOR OF GOD is not a metaphor. I think most people have a vague notion about it, not realizing that the armor is a real thing. You are actually putting on real combat gear in the spirit realm; it is just as real as God, whom you cannot see. This is not symbolic; but actual equipment provided for your well-being.

Ephesians 6:10-18 Finally, my brethren, be strong in the Lord and in the power of his might. Put on the whole armor of God, that you may be able to stand against the wiles of the devil. For we wrestle not against flesh and blood, but against principalities, against powers, against the rulers of the darkness of this world [or age], against spiritual wickedness in high places. Wherefore take unto you the whole armor of God that you may be able to withstand in the evil day, and having done all, to stand. Stand therefore, having your loins girt about with truth, and having on the breastplate of righteousness; and your feet shod with the preparation of the gospel of peace, above all, taking the shield of faith, wherewith you shall be able to quench all the fiery darts of the wicked. And take the helmet of salvation, and the sword of the Spirit, which is the word of God. Praying always with all prayer and supplications in the Spirit and watching [being alert] thereunto with all perseverance and supplications for all saints.

In this one illustration Paul used the following: Wrestling, wiles (meaning devious strategy), armor, standing (as in battle won) breastplate, shoes, shield, fiery darts (the evil one flings "fiery darts" at us daily to knock us off balance, or over the precipice. You will no doubt be bombarded by thousands of fiery arrows launched by Satan and his minions. The only way to protect yourself is through faith. Apostle John wrote, "This is the victory that has overcome the world – our faith" (I John 5:4)

Quite interestingly, I've found that in every place where the scriptures speak about spiritual warfare it is always in conjunction with teaching about relationships. What I found was eye-opening! We have been trying to claim Ephesians 6:10 for instance: *"Finally, my brethren, be strong in the Lord"* - without doing the things that precede the "finally." Most of Ephesians deals with relationships in the home, in marriage, and in the church. If the enemy has a foothold in any of these areas it must be dealt with before we can ever wrestle against principalities and powers. Any right that we try to hold onto will be played upon by the enemy of our souls in time of battle. The right to be offended. The right to our time. The right to do what we want with our possessions, the right to self-pity, the right to self-justification, self-righteousness, self-willed. Upon yielding to the Holy Spirit, He will convict you of any issues in your life that He is not pleased with.

As previously stated, the first place to go to battle is on a personal level. It is important to close up all the holes in our own armor that might let the enemy come in and hit us. We can stand and quote the verse all day that "a curse without cause shall not alight (Proverbs 26:2)." But we do not always realize that strongholds in our own lives make us susceptible to the enemy.

It is not two months down the road, or five months down the road. The battle that comes to you and me is not prophetically down the road of time. It is right here and right now. Right now, is always the perfect time to prepare. Why? Because, when Satan attacks, you won't have time to google or ask Siri to help you locate your spiritual armor. You must be prepared.

We first accept our Protection from Christ. (EPHESIANS 6)

This combat equipment provided by Him for our use, is "the full armor of God" (Ephesians 6:11,13) All pieces of equipment serve for defensive warfare except for only one which is for offensive warfare.

Brief Summary of Spiritual Weapons:

The belt of truth (:14). The function of this belt served as the foundation of which the sword, knife or dagger was attached to the waist of the roman soldier, much like the belt of today, so truth must encompass our whole life (Psalm 51:6; John 8:32). There must be no middle ground, no hypocrisy, negotiating, or compromise.

The breastplate of righteousness (:14). The function of the breastplate served to cover and protect the vital organs of the soldier. We are to remain standing firm in Christ who is our righteousness. Remaining in right standing with Christ in our lives.

The shoes of preparation (:15). Paul tells us that our readiness for battle is the good news of Jesus life, death and resurrection. (Isaiah 26: 3).

The shield of faith (:16). The function of the shield is to protect each part of our body by extinguishing the flaming arrows of the enemy. Faith must operate in respect to each part of our life. We trust in Jesus alone as our shield.

The helmet of salvation (:17). Protection for the head, neck and shoulders. Paul's use of the word "salvation" denotes that the helmet serves as a source of complete deliverance.

The sword of the Spirit (:17). Paul tells us the sword represents the word of God. God's word is a powerful weapon. (Hebrews 4:12 and Matthew 4)

We must Pray to maintain our Communion and Fellowship with Christ (:18). This is essential for victory. Praying always, all prayer, in all seasons, with all perseverance."

Dressed for Battle Prayer

Lord, by faith here's what I'm doing.... I'm putting on the girdle of truth...Help me to walk in truth today.

I'm putting on the breastplate of righteousness...Help me to guard my emotions.

I'm putting on the boots of preparation to be ready to stand firm in my relationship with you because I have peace in you.

I'm taking the shield of faith...I'm gonna trust you God for everything. I declare Satan is defeated every time he fires a fiery dart at me; it will be deflected by my Shield of Faith.

I'm putting on the helmet of salvation....to guard my thoughts and thinking. Don't let me think the wrong things.

And Father, I'm taking the sword of the spirit.... your precious word, and I pray you would bring it to my mind anytime I get tempted, tried or tested.

Today, I walk in complete Victory as a Well-Armed Solider of the Son of the Living God.

Amen.

THE UNDERMINING CULPRIT - GREED

John Steinbeck's The Pearl. It's the story of a happy, but poor, pearl diver who dreams of finding the perfect pearl. One day he finds it, but rather than bringing him the happiness he had hoped for, it brings him one problem after another, because everyone is after his pearl. He almost gets killed. His son is killed. He and his wife are at odds. His formerly tranquil life is totally upset because of his attempts to cling to this pearl. Finally, he stands at the shore and hurls the cursed pearl as far into the sea as he can. That's what we must do with our greed! Radically separate yourself from it! Put it to death! "For it is because of these things that the wrath of God will come!"

Webster defines it as "excessive or reprehensible acquisitiveness." It defines the synonym, "covetous," as, "marked by inordinate desire for wealth or possessions or for another's possessions." The problem is those terms are subjective. Most of us would say, "I don't have excessive, reprehensible, inordinate desires! I would just like a little bit more" (and more, and more)! A greedy person has twins named "Gimme" and Gimme more."

Sadly, in my work culture, it seems a norm to witness a fairly quiet work climate drastically shift to hostility and long-lasting relationships disintegrate due to resentment and jealousy. In addition to observing Christians displaying ungodly traits as the most ruthless, undermining culprit take on the spirit of greed mostly always over one lil word, "Overtime"!

Greed is never quite satisfied. Greed breeds financial disputes. We see this in the parable Jesus told in Luke 12:13-21.

Someone out of the crowd said, "Teacher, order my brother to give me a fair share of the family inheritance."

Thinking wwjd (what would Jesus do)? I would have expected Jesus to say, "Don't worry, I'll deal with that selfish scoundrel!"

But rather Jesus replied, "Mister, what makes you think it's any of my business to be a judge or mediator for you?" (:14) Speaking to the people, he went on, "Take care! Protect yourself against the least bit of greed. Life is not defined by what you have, even when you have a lot." (:15)

Then Jesus told them this story (:16-19 paraphrased) relating to the farm of a certain rich man that had excessively more than enough crops for his already overflowing barns. He began talking and reasoning with himself. Praising himself, patting himself on the back for his material abundance. "What can I do? My barn isn't big enough for this harvest. Then he said, "Here's what I'll do: I'll tear down my barns and build bigger ones to stockpile for the future. Then I'll gather in all my grain and goods, and I'll say to myself, Self, you've done well! You've got it made and can now retire. Take it easy and have the time of your life!"

In critically thinking about this passage, the rich farmer is not said to have gained his wealth illegally or by taking advantage of others. He could very well be one thought of as securing his future. However, the farmer became preoccupied with self-absorption. Beware of such inner conversations that announces the unholy trinity of the three personal pronouns:

"me, myself and I". Beware not to fall prey of worshipping self. This three-fold cord is not easily broken.

In verse (:20), the farmer is described and addressed a question: "Fool!" Tonight, you die. And your barn full of goods-who gets it?' The farmer was not called "fool" because of his wealth or ambition. He was not called "fool" for saving for a rainy day. He was called "fool" because he equated finite things with an infinite value. I believe we too as the rich farmer are culturally challenged in overcoming the seduction of possessions in many ways. Jesus concluded (:21), "That's what happens when you fill your barn with Self and not with God."

Even though the farmer had plenty, he was by far from being satisfied. The more he had, the more he wanted. No thought of gratitude or benevolence of blessing others was ever expressed. That's the signification of greed. A greedy person is an idolater, and greed brings the wrath of God. (Colossians 3:5)

Greed will also rob you of contentment and cause such discouragement that you don't believe God wants to bless you. So, you blame God, you blame the boss, you blame the payroll system or whatever system you deem responsible –

and yet the responsible party is you. Could it be you have violated scriptural principles with your unbridled spending?

A few relating scriptures are Colossians 3:5, Ephesians 5:5, and 1 Corinthians 5:10-11 which tells us not to associate with anyone who claims to be a Christian but is greedy – not even to eat with such people.

Viewing wealth by God's standards?

Wealth is not sin. All wealth comes from God as a gift and is a responsibility and accountability to use it well and do good.

"Tell those rich in this world's wealth to quit being so full of themselves and so obsessed with money, which is here today and gone tomorrow. Tell them to go after God, who piles on all the riches we could ever manage – to do good, to be rich in helping others, to be extravagantly generous. If they do that, they'll build a treasury that will last, gaining life that is truly life." (I Timothy 6:17-18 MSG)

Psalm 24:1 declares: "The earth is the Lord's and everything in it, the world, and all who lives in it."

Everything belongs to God, and as stewards of God's gifts, we are to manage the possessions entrusted to us in ways that honor Him.

Now for the convicting part of this subject matter. Here are some questions to help you take your spiritual pulse with regard to greed. The truth of the matter is – we all wrestle with a beast called "self" and therefore this assessment requires an open and honest deep search of the heart before the throne of God.

- How can I know if I'm greedy?

- Why do I want more money?

- Will I betray my co-workers for a bit of extra money?

- Do I compete to work the most overtime hours in the office?

- Is overtime or extra jobs necessary to care of my family?

- How does the extra work for money affect my health?

- How does the time away from family affect those relationships?

- Will I jeopardize key relationships over money differences?

- What will I do if I win the lottery?

While biblical principles do apply, there are no hard and fast rules to guide in every situation. Before giving further consideration to these indicators, let's be careful to judge ourselves and not others (Matthew 7:1-5) This assessment is on a personal level. However, if you think that another Christian is being deceived by greed, your responsibility is gently to seek to restore him. (Galatians 6:1)

The Basic Stewardship Checkup

Am I valuing souls above earthly things?" If I rejoice when I win a raffle, a door prize, or a lottery, but I yawn when I hear about a soul being saved, I've lost the eternal perspective, which is a sign of greed.

Why do I want more money?

This is a question about motives. Do I want more to provide more adequately for my family? That may be legitimate. But if I want more just to buy bigger and better stuff that I really don't need, I may be drifting into greed. If I knew that I were to die in one year, would I do anything different in my management of God's resources? Would I buy this item? Would I give more to His cause?

Am I more concerned about making money than I am about? my eternal destiny?

This is the question Jesus raised in the parable of the man who wanted to build bigger barns. He was laying up treasure for himself on earth, but he wasn't rich toward God. I realize that it takes a lot of time and energy to earn a living. And there's nothing wrong with working hard to succeed in your career. But if my every waking moment is consumed with how to succeed financially and I seldom think about how I can succeed at seeking first God's kingdom and righteousness, I'm probably tainted by greed.

What is the source of my security: my job, money or God?

Be careful with this one! We all know the "right" answer.

But what if all my things, my bank accounts, everything was taken from me; Could I trust God if, like Job, I lost everything?

How much do I mourn the loss of money and things?

If I'm considering buying something, how hard would it be for me to give this up later? My level of grief when I lose something is directly proportional to my emotional attachment to that thing. It's normal to grieve when we lose something of value, whether a possession or money. But if we're trusting the Lord and recognizing that all we have belongs to Him, we shouldn't be devastated. If we are, we may be greedy.

Do I compromise godly character or priorities in the pursuit of making money?

Some things ought to count far more than making money: God's reputation through my testimony as a Christian; my relationship with Jesus Christ; a clear conscience; my relationship with my family and others. If I'm willing to shred relationships or to take advantage of another person for financial gain, I'm being greedy.

Am I prone to get-rich quick schemes?

If I feel myself drawn to some easy, instant way to making a fortune, I probably need to deal with my greed. This includes gambling and playing the lottery. I admit that it can be tempting when the Powerball gets into hundreds of millions, but gambling is poor stewardship of the Lord's resources.

Am I in bondage to credit cards and debt?

I realize that some are in debt because of being out of work or because of unavoidable hardship. I'm not talking about that. But most people who are in debt have a problem with overspending. That's a sign of greed!

If these questions have uncovered some seeds of greed, then consider the final question:

How can I deal with my greed?

I must radically separate myself from all greed, beginning on the thought level.

Learn to walk in the Spirit so that His fruit of self-control governs your impulses.

To rid yourself of greed, make a faith commitment to give generously to the Lord's work. Giving is the drain plug for greed. If you say, "If I just made more, I'd give more," you're probably fooling yourself. Why not trust God and increase the percentage you give now? When you get an increase in income, rather than automatically spending or giving unwisely -Ask God and obey where He wants you to direct it.

September 28, 2011 was an extraordinary day of divine revelation for me regarding a spiritual law. I was meditating on Ecclesiastes 11 when the Holy Spirit began ministering to me:

"SEEDTIME".

"Cast thy bread upon the water; for thou shalt find it after many days. Give a portion to seven, and also eight; for thou knowest not what evil shall be upon the earth. If the clouds be full of rain, they empty themselves upon the earth and if the tree fall toward the south, or toward the north, in the place where the tree falleth, there it shall be." (Ecclesiastes 11:1-6)

I understand this WORD to imply this: Don't insist on having a perfect time before you start doing what God has laid on your heart to do and has given you approval to start doing. If you insist, you'll never achieve anything! Your destiny will never speak. It will remain a piece of paper, and your life will never bless anyone. I began asking the Lord to whom, and where was I to give or to sow. In obedience, I began sowing into different ventures, causes and ministries as He directed. We usually want a guaranteed outcome before we tend to make a move. But the truth of the matter is this: It's in those times of uncertainty that tries our resolve, prove our faith, and test our courage.

I am an extravagant giver that looks for opportunities to give as led of the Lord. Since the time of that revelation on seedtime and harvest/ sowing & reaping, I've seen the provision of the Lord increased mightily upon me and my family's life, where I'm not only blessed, but I'm blessed to be a blessing.

You can never beat God's giving so whenever, to whomever, and whatever He impresses upon you to give – Just do it! No matter how small or insignificant you may think it is, don't ever let that be the issue. The key is OBEDIENCE! **Don't ever Underestimate Your seed that's given in Obedience!**

I also encourage you to always pray over your seed before you release it. Learn to give it an assignment because it carries the potential to bring wholeness in every realm – not only financially; but physically, emotionally and spiritually.

Overcome greed by repenting if you have not always obeyed God's commands in your finances

Overcome greed by making Jesus the Master of your heart and finances.

Overcome greed by being faithful in giving your tithes and offerings.

And the Lord will deal with every stronghold that has developed against your supply line!

THE UNDERMINING CULPRIT – ENVY/JEALOUSY

Several months ago, after my morning devotion in prayer, I heard the word "jealousy". Immediately I began soul-searching "me," asking the Lord to Search Me and to Sit on the Throne of my Heart as a Refiner and a Purifier. I also began doing a basic study on the word. Nothing elaborate —-just definitions, meaning of the word, identifying the sub-ruling spirits, defining the difference between jealousy and envy and if the difference really matters?

Both ENVY and JEALOUSY are self-inflicted negative emotions. Jealousy is the emotional desire to keep for yourself what rightfully belongs to you. Envy is the emotional desire to have for yourself what rightfully belongs to another.

Envy is always sinful. Jealousy in some circumstances, as in marital infidelity is an obvious example. Jealousy is both entirely natural and entirely appropriate, as much as it needs to be handled very carefully. And this is why the difference matters:

You shall worship no other God; For I the Lord thy God am a Jealous God. (Exodus20:5). So, for the Bible to say that God is envious would be to imply that there is something He wants that He does not have. But to say that He is jealous is to say that there is something He has (you and I) that He does not want to lose.

So, do you see the difference? Envy and Jealousy are different; and Yes, it matters how we handle these emotions.

During the course of this study, the Holy Spirit brought to my remembrance a specific occurrence of nearly two years ago that involved jealousy against me and my family. What do you do after learning that someone is jealous of you? How do you respond to the spiritual attack of jealousy? I used to just chalk it up and say "Well, that's on them, they gotta answer for that. We're all gonna reap what we sow!"

Well, as I was preparing to minister earlier this year; the Lord led me deeper into the study of this matter and I discovered the following: Jealousy is a destructive spirit that falls under the "works of the flesh."

It makes one under-mind circumstances and people. It causes anger, a divided mind, insecurity, losing focus on your own life, and getting easily offended. We lose relationships because of jealousy. It causes fear and we know that fear has torment. The worst thing jealousy brings is that it leads to sin. And that sin if not repented, leads to death. Someone consumed with jealousy and rage will kill because they cannot control the envy that is within them. Do you know that even most physical ailments are caused by envy, bitterness, and jealousy?

When a child of God desires something influenced by the Spirit, it works as a prayer going to God. Things moving; being activated in the invisible realm for that believer. Likewise, in the same way, when a person (even if it's a believer) allows jealousy to function through him/her, he is then opening his spirit to be influenced by the principalities of the world. He then becomes a messenger of the devil.

A jealous Christian is the same as a witch /warlock. A jealous Christian becomes a messenger of the devil; because when you are jealous your wish synchronizes with the enemy's plans to destroy the person, you're jealous of. This is Spiritual Warfare!

I come as an OVERCOMER to further expose this strongman of jealousy in example of displacement. Somebody has either been displaced or thinks they might be displaced by a coming change. This example of "Displacement" is what I believe to be the root issue in terms of Jealousy. Psalm 8:3-5 says: *"When I consider your heavens, the work of your fingers, the moon, and the stars, which you have set in place, What is man that you are mindful of him, the son of man that you care for him? You made him a little lower than the heavenly beings and crowned him with glory and honor."*

Beloved, we have wanted the devil use to have. The enemy is jealous of the God-given position we now have. Therefore, whenever another individual becomes jealous of you, all of the hatred that Satan feels towards you because of his displacement issues can flow through that individual to you with deadly force! They become the pipeline through which the toxic hatred of hell can be pumped into your life.

So, yes, a persons' jealousy of another person's success and blessing can very well shut doors and cause downfall. And we need to be conscious in our spirits and in our hearts of the proper response to this attack. You must not walk around in a daze being oblivious to the things of the Spirit. Live conscious in the spirit and pray against such destructive forces. Ask the Lord to give you the grace to be sensitive to the things of the Spirit, grace to love your enemies, and grace to overcome such attacks.

THE UNDERMINING CULPRIT
JEZEBEL/AHAB (Kings I and 2)

The tool this spirit uses is manipulation. Devising wickedness in your heart against others, stopping at nothing to get what they want, even if it means lie, cheat, steal, even kill. In 1 Kings 21, we learn that King Ahab would pout when he did not get his own way. He had seen a vineyard that he greatly desired, but the owner would not give up his precious property, even to the king. As King Ahab lay on his bed sulking, Jezebel assured him she would get him what he wanted. Jezebel is a strongman's name for a spirit of control. This spirit is a total control freak, and it is also very good at manipulation and getting people to do its evil bidding.

If you sense this spirit is at work in your workplace, it is important to see the enemy as spiritual, not fleshly. Don't hate the person being controlled by the spirit of Jezebel. Recognize that it is a spiritual power - one that God must fight. Let your prayer be: *"O our God, will You not judge them? For we have no power against this great multitude that is coming against us; nor do we know what to do, but our eyes are upon You" (2 Chr. 20:12).*

I share the following with you in how to recognize this spirit in your midst, whether it be at home, within your family, in church, in ministry or at your workplace;

Let's first debunk several misconceptions about Jezebel.

Jezebel is not a demon spirit solely assigned to women. Jezebel is a spirit, not a gender. Jezebel's agenda is more extensive than just ungodly control and manipulation.

A person can have a spirit of control without having a Jezebel spirit. However, a Jezebel spirit will always have a spirit of control. This spirit has been attacking mankind ever since Adam and Eve were cast out of the Garden of Eden. Until Jesus comes back to set up His Millennium Kingdom and throws Satan and all of his demons into the bottomless pit, we are all going to be stuck with this kind of evil spirit being allowed to roam in the air seeking the next victim it will attack and devour.

Looking back over the six encounters I have had with this spirit, four of which occurred in the workplace and two within the church setting. The one specific thing I have noticed is that this spirit is actually easy to spot after a certain length of time. In other words, it keeps playing the same types of games every time it moves in on a person or a situation.

For example, a spirit of anger will only try to make you mad and angry, but a Jezebel spirit will play a number of different games with you to bring you down, as you will discover during the reading of this segment and even more so throughout the subsequent chapters.

When you think about the world and who gets what they want, they are usually people who will get angry, raise their voice, add some base to their tone, manipulate, demand, argue for hours and wear you down until you give in to their demands. They whine until they get their way. Then after all that - if they still don't get their way, they will lie about you to people who have influence over you to discredit you. This is all to put pressure on you to get you to break so you will give in to their demands. Do you know any people like this in the world?

Those who are more the aggressor, demanding, angry, prideful, controlling is classified as the spirit of Jezebel. Jezebel involves many other demons that report to it including, fear, control, lying, manipulation, anger, jealousy, sexual perversion and pride (which comes from the spirit of Leviathan in Job 41). When the spirit of Jezebel begins to manifest, it seeks a high seat or a place of dominance.

Below I have identified some specific things about this spirit once it moves in on someone within a territory or region to set up shop; and its' consequences:

Speaks Evil, Critical Words, Evil Decrees

"I HATE YOU" - The word curse of Jezebel is loaded with toxic spiritual venom that unleashes a negative imagery. Elijah could see what she wanted to do to him. He saw her hate and rage towards him. He saw her bloodthirsty plans of death for his life. This sight and sound experience opened a gateway of despair.

The Webbing Network Analogy

Spider Webs are intriguing to me for their capability of flexibility and depth. As the spider engineers its handiwork of webbing, it is notably impactful when constructed well.

On a behavioral level, our network of relationship with others also serve in the formation of a web in the ability to draw people with a compelling charm. Likewise of a jezebel spirit, it lures people into its well-spun webs without them ever realizing what has occurred. It then moves in for the attack to completely destroy.

Seeks to connect to Clever, Astute, Attractive and Resourceful People

This spirit likes to target these kinds of people because it wants it all. It wants total control of everything; and therefore, prides in being the center of all attention. Although cleverly disguised, on center stage is where you will spot this spirit in operation.

Seeks to Infiltrate, Intrude, and Sabotage Everything

Once this spirit has maneuvered its way in, it then seeks to gradually and slyly gain access to it all. It is very good at playing mind games with people. It is a mastermind of smooth talk with persuasive power.

Another thing this spirit skillfully devises in doing is causing a lot of tic for tack fighting, backbiting, and malicious type gossiping among the people that are caught in its web. This spirit hates civility, repentance, and true holiness.

Ferociously attacks any type of leadership position

Elders, Pastors, Priest, Youth Pastor, Deacons, Praise &Worship Team Leaders, Organist, Sound Engineers, Head of Households, Supervisors, Upper level management of business sectors and other platforms of authority. These leadership titles were just to name a few but understand NO LEADER OF ANY ENTITY IS EXEMPT. Jezebel prefers refined qualities but will use anyone to dislodge out of the service and the calling of the Lord.

Spews False and Deceptive

This kind of deceptiveness has the ability to unseat and displace you from office by infiltrating false imagery, perceptions, prophecies, dreams and visions. Matthew 7:15 warns us about the false prophets dressed as a sheep approach; but are actually devouring wolves. Scripture also cautions us that all prophecies are to be weighed, discerned and judged. (1John 4:1)

Primarily Hates Prophets, any form of Prayer, and Spiritual Warfare

Just as Queen Jezebel in the Old Testament hated the prophets of God, this spirit also has an abhorrence for Prayer Warriors and Prayer which is the genetic make-up of my spiritual DNA{**as a prayer strategist and spiritual sniper**} The submitted prayer life of a believer that yields to the Spirit of God; praying forth the will and the purposes of the Father, praying for the establishment of the Kingdom of God in the earth is understandably the reason for the attack on many prayer lives by this vicious spirit.

The Deceived Host is unable to recognize this spirit in them

Because this spirit is rooted in darkness and evil; it masquerades and camouflages itself; and thus, without the presence of the Holy Spirit, the carrying host will not recognize they are giving a place for such wickedness to thrive in and through them.

Other identified evil traits of the Jezebel Spirit:

- Looks to establish its' own alliance.
- Preys on the weakness and vulnerability of others
- See itself as always right with an already excuse for its behavior, no matter how outrageous it may be. Blames others by playing the victims' card and falsely accusing everyone else.
- Fixated with high-ranking positions/titles of prominence that can help to establish its' base of influence in reaching its' goals and agendas in whatever terrain or territory it is seeking to dominate. Keeps their true identity concealed especially from its' targets.
- With little to no assessing much of anything, this spirit makes ill-intent promises and uses the ideas and good-will proposals of others to gain impressive honors of the upper echelon.

- Strategically divides to conquer as it secretly and conniving put people at odds with one another behind the scenes.

This spirit graphically constitutes: Vile, Pure Evil and Hate, Pride, Lustful and Seductive, Self-Centered and Narcissistic, Judgmental, Critical, Condescending, and Demeaning, Overly Demanding and Manipulating, Ruthless, Cunning and Calculation, Combative and Confrontational, Lying and Cheating, Cannot stand any type of Constructive Criticism.

Encountering such a spirit or working in close proximity to this kind of evil spirit, regardless of location – be it at your place of worship, place of business, place of socialization, or within the confines of your home. In most instances, as I stated earlier, the person hosting this evil-natured spirit has been seduced and blind-sided and is clueless of its impact. Depending on the length of time that has passed between something once being a "foothold" having now become a "stronghold", could gravely be the difference in the manner of approach. I strongly suggest in such extreme cases, go directly to God the Father and get His divine plan of action on how to proceed. Pray that God will supernaturally show them that they really do have this kind of spirit operating on the inside of them and that He reveals the mode of deliverance specifically for them.

Also, in connection to the spirit of Jezebel operating, you will usually also find an "Ahab" nearby, or someone in leadership who is allowing the Jezebel spirit access and control as they tend to feel more comfortable with people who have no issues taking the ball and running with it, usurp authority in making decisions; especially as it relates to challenging disciplinary issues in the workplace. "Ahab's" thrives on relinquishing its' authority over to Jezebel." Unfortunately, those decisions are always against the purposes and plans of the Lord.

Ahab Characteristics includes:

- Does not like confrontation
- Afraid of being rejected so will go along with whatever stronger personalities demand
- Avoids telling people what needs to be said for correction due to fear of an argument
- Worried what other people will think of them
- Believe you should always act happy in spite of feeling controlled and dominated
- Very nice person but too nice as you let people do things that you should stand up to

- Will do anything to gain acceptance

Don't let Jezebel be the Boss of You'

A sure sign that this spirit has infiltrated your workplace will be the evidence of much strife, dissension, and chaos – causing mass mutiny and disloyalty, along with seriously affecting the productivity of your entire work force. This spirit and the person who is carrying it are toxic, and they will infect and contaminate every person they come into major contact with, as this kind of spirit is an attack dog and will viciously attack anyone who will get too close to it.

When the spirit of Jezebel begins to manifest in the business world, it seeks a high seat of authority or a place of dominance. Usually it will manifest in someone who wants to teach or lead, or wants access to classified information and to be linked to important people of "titles" so to appear more than what and who they are – all in the forming of an alliance to lure its host into their web. Have you ever recognized someone blatantly going around the office looking over their shoulders as they are whispering maliciousness; or discreetly "sowing discord" whereby their facial expression, hand gestures, and body language tells it all; or "loudly expressing" themselves in a hostile manner? I've seen this type of foul behavior in real life many times in the workplace and it must not be condoned. If the devil is trying to sow discord – you should know he's on an assignment - Don't be deceived!

If you do not contend against such viciousness, this spirit will set up shop. You cannot give any ground to this kind of evil spirit. If you do, it will establish a stronghold base within your surroundings; and from there, it will launch attacks on both you and anyone else that is in this environment.

I thought it quite interesting that one article stated Jezebel has a distinct sound when formulated into an outburst or a laugh. "It sounds similar to a witch-like cackle." Have you ever heard such outbursts? Begin to pay attention and become sensitive to your surrounding sounds.

Remember, in such extreme cases, go directly to God the Father and get His divine plan of action on how to proceed. It's a life of obedience that throws this wickedness down to its death – not just talk!

CHAPTER 6

PULLING BACK THE CURTAINS
(MY BACKSTAGE WORK EXPERIENCES)

EXPOSING UNDERCOVER PERSONNEL

If you have been lied to, lied about, ostracized, attacked, or maligned by hell. If you have been under siege by the accusing and assailing powers of hell, then these upcoming closing chapters will be found both insightful and liberating. One of the primary tools in the arsenal of hell is lying accusations. The enemy and his minions relentlessly hurl accusations at the life of a believer. People often make false accusations against ministries and those doing the work of God. These accusations are rarely founded upon truth and almost always uttered undercover in darkness. One way that you can discern the spirit behind this is how it is handled. Does the person making the accusation share it with the one they are accusing as the Bible instructs? Most of the time, the answer is no, because it is simply a ploy of the devil to discourage, distract, and divide.

Be ushered in a new level of freedom as you're enlightened by *"My Backstage Work Experiences"* in contending against some of the most undermining culprits: Greed, Jealousy, Jezebel and more....

He who vindicates Me is near; Who will contend with Me? Let us stand up to each other; Who has a case against Me? Let him draw near to Me. (Isaiah 50:8)

The word vindicate means, to free from allegation or blame, confirm, substantiate, provide justification or defense for, to protect from attack or encroachment, to defend or avenge. It also means to set free and deliver!

This definition paints a vivid picture of the supernatural defense of the Lord. He desires to free you from every hellish allegation and lie. He also desires to confirm your destiny and assignment. In the freedom that God brings, He acquits you from every charge and absolves you. The vindication of Heaven is powerful and swift. It comes suddenly and miraculously undoing the lies of the wicked one.

OVERCOMING PERSECUTION

We are constantly engaged in intense spiritual warfare as the accuser of the brethren is always trying to make a name for himself by defaming us. The study of 1 Corinthians 4:13 helped me to understand how to respond to the numerous

in the way of consolation and encouragement. It also implies an effort to persuade or to overcome resistance.

Now, let's bring both words together to understand the revelation behind Paul's response in handling himself in such matters. *"Being defamed, we entreat...."* Being bashed by defamation of character, did he retaliate? Did he seek revenge? Did he become bitter and offended? Did he become angry and react aggressively against his attackers? Did he respond by waging a counterattack?

Well, maybe not Paul, but I've personally, most certainly have wanted to satisfy the craving of my flesh tempting me to put people in their place once and for all! It is undeniably an uncomfortable feeling to know that people are saying shameful and dishonorable things about you that are simply untrue. However, we all must come to know the indispensable lesson that you must not blow up in a damaging way despite the pettiness and entitlement that surrounds us.

We see that Paul grasped the intuitive understanding of "entreat" by associating with his core group.

"Bad company corrupts good character" (1 Cor. 15:33), which is why the caliber of people you surround yourself with will either have a positive or negative impact on your choice of response. This testifies to the company you keep with your thoughts which is heavily influenced by the things we see and hear.

"Being defamed, we entreat....". *When we are* victimized by such cruel attacks is the time to lock arms together with your team of support for strength, consolation and encouragement.

Paul's words in First Corinthians 4:13 could be interpreted: "When people assault our integrity, our character, or our name, we begin to exhort and encourage one another...." trust God to vindicate your name and character.

Had I taken the approach to retaliate against my accusers, it probably would have stirred the waters and made the situation much more turbulent. This was the first type of major attacks against me in the work arena; but certainly not the last! I've had to come under much weight of persecution and scrutiny, and javelins being thrown at me without knowing why; until I began to understand the root causes of the driving force.

Learning to take the 1Corinthians 4:13 approach helped me stay on track regardless of what people said, did, or wrote about me. However, prior to this download of revelation knowledge, I would love to tell you that of approx. 250 accusations within a ten-year tenure, most of those were directed to general management as a whole but many were individually directed to me. I would love to tell you that I responded to all of them in the 1 Corinthians 4:13 manner described above – but sad to say: "That will be a negative"!!

I failed the test many times due to my improper response(s) while trying to prove my innocence and defend myself, and as a result, I was hindered in moving forth in my endeavor to overcome this level of opposition.

You must first become established in the truth of your identity as it relates to your purpose and kingdom assignment. Then you'll begin to govern yourself from heaven's perspective:

"Ok God – You're allowing things to come at me and Why? What is it that you're trying to strengthen me in? Which attribute of the Fruit of the Spirit needs perfecting in me? What part of me that is emotionally not ready to sit in the office of the kingship?"

You see, you will continually be tested in the area of your imperfection until you pass the test. The quicker you learn not to take these vindictive, character assassination attacks personally – the quicker you pass the test of spiritual maturity. You must conclude: "It is business. Kingdom Business." When God promotes you to a higher level of responsibility, He calls you to a deeper level of submission. "Humble yourself before the Lord, and He will lift you up." Submission brings strength. It's the submitted life that has the power to OVERCOME.

In each case filed against me, God gracefully equipped me to overcome each barrier, and opposition hurled at me in my path. I am grateful to God to say that **not** half of them, **not** few of them; but **not** a single one of charges against me was ever found valid or with any substance. They all were dismissed. I escaped every trap of the enemy. How ironic! Every ditch dug for me by my accusers had been dug strategically and preserved for each of them.

If you have ever experienced situations of this nature, do not be lured into an emotional battle by the devil. Instead, allow your core group members to exhort and encourage you to be faithful in guarding your heart against such offense.

Relationships are key. When you are "defamed," it is time to "entreat"; reminding one another, "This is warfare!" Let's go deeper to uncover more of the enemy's devices:

- Both Python and Leviathan are twisting serpent spirits. They will twist what you hear. They will try to seed your heart with wounds and offenses to cripple you.

- Demons do not want powerful Kingdom connections! They understand that alignment with the right people can unlock the power of God. Agreement is powerful. The spirit of accusation comes to break unity and agreement; and that's why the enemy doesn't care if we fight each other. Just as long as we're not targeting (him) the real enemy. Do not fight wars you are not called to fight. Fighting in the flesh when your place of victory is in the spirit. Pray and ask the Lord for power and discernment to fight the right enemy and to cultivate unity in the relationships He's entrusted to you.

- We can judge things and we can measure scenarios, but if we are going to seek peace in our hearts, we must allow the Lord to vindicate us, to fight for us, and to speak on our behalf.

- Don't yield to the temptation to fight fleshly wars. The enemy is trying to pull you into unauthorized warfare. He knows if he can pull you out of the realm of the spirit and into the flesh, then he can conquer you. This is his goal, to stir you up and get you into sin. He wants to get your mouth running wild and your mind racing. He wants to get you over in the flesh. There are times when accusation arises that the Lord will tell you to keep silent. It makes no sense but in those moments of deep surrender you are learning to truly trust Him, and you will prevail in the end.

We must be good soldiers and be faithful to the end regardless of what people say or do to us!

It is El Channun who bears the right to judge and the right to show grace.

Declare Supernatural Justice and Unusual Vindication over your situation at hand!

OVERCOMING THE VICIOUS ROAR OF ACCUSATIONS

Persuasion versus Manipulation

I find it necessary to broadly define the difference between the terms persuasion and manipulation as to identify with the forthcoming schemes and strategies of the enemy as he is exposed. Over a period of years, I've spent a huge amount of time and energy studying human nature and the way that we process arguments and facts. Although there's a fine line between persuasion and manipulation, the most obvious difference is motive or intent. Manipulation implies persuasion with the intent to fool, control or contrive the person on the other side of the conversation that leaves them either harmed or without benefit. Perhaps, persuasion plants seeds while manipulation is focused on harvest?

(Chosen to Stand Unmoved!)

In studying the book of Daniel, we can't miss its relevance to our own day – a collapsing culture, egotistical leaders, a chaotic work climate. Here were four young men whose testimony has been a source of strength to every saint facing a temptation.

In paraphrasing Daniel 6:1-28 – Belok, Kamur and Daniel were the three governors under the rule ship of King Darius. Belok and Kamur were summoned by King Darius to justify the grievances and charges relating to government corruption and fraud within their presiding areas.

Their plan of action entailed launching towards a more aggressive and forceful approach to resolve the situation. King Darius also wanted to know why he had not received any complaints from Daniel's provinces.

Kamur replied, "Don't think he's all that! He isn't as smart and honest as you think. We have the inside story that he has discharged most of the officials you've appointed for his sector.

(I sense jealousy brewing!)

"Oh, is that so? Well, let's also bring in Daniel to answer the charge being bought against him." Daniel was escorted in.

(Check out the irate-toned false allegations)

Darius states: "Daniel, you have been charged with dismissing more than half of your allocated officials within your sector. Please explain."

"My king, I didn't dismiss them. They freely chose to resign rather than accept my terms of leadership. I demanded strict responsible accountability."

Belok was furious. He yelled, "Preposterous! This is beyond all reason. Totally absurd! What kinda person would suggest such a harebrained notion!"

(Oh, how I love Daniel's wise response!)

Daniel keeps his composure, unruffled as he responds to his critics. Darius asks, "Daniel, why don't you apply assertiveness in being more forceful and aggressive in your dealings, as the other governors do?"

Daniel replied. "Listening always awakens awareness. Change is certain and peace is followed by disturbances when we effectively communicate our thought processes in a trusting manner. The meeting of the minds benefits both parties resulting in a win-win situation and eliminates the need for severe or forceful discipline."

(Honored in the presence of your enemies)

Darius sternly says to Belok and Kamur. "Effective immediately, this is the example you are to emulate!" Daniel was favored by the king and granted an on the spot promotion as the king ended the meeting.

(Oh, be careful guys ...Touch not Thine Anointed!)

Belok was fire hot as he retorted, "I can't stand him," "I'm gonna get him", I've gotta find a way to discredit him". I'm not going out like this! This is not how all this is gonna end! I'm next in line for promotion and I will not be out-smarted or out-ranked. No Siree!

They hated Daniel. The two conspirators privately met for the next several days to devise evil against him. They hired spies, paid off servants in the palace to eavesdrop on all of Daniel's conversations.

(No Weapon Formed...Shall Prosper)

After months of intense surveillance, none of the private investigators could find anything against Daniel, until at last one of the servants reported seeing a woman visiting Daniel's house in the night hours. Belok questioned Haban, the guard in Daniel's home. "What's this thing being done in the dark between Daniel and the mysterious woman that visits his private chambers?" "No, my lord," Haban replied. "Daniel is only being generous to this recently widowed Jew by giving her some money to help support her needs. This is not an unusual thing for him to do."

Oh, how well I can identify with this scenario as it relates to offering a helping hand in private to those in need. Some of these time-sensitive and personal matters are often misconstrued and taken out of context especially by those with evil eyes who are constantly monitoring your every move.

(Daniel remains steadfast in prayer)

After all was said and done, the two men concluded Daniel's only unusual behavior was that he prays to his God three times a day come rain or shine. Suddenly, an evil plot of deception was erected from the wickedness of Belok's heart to manipulate the king into issuing an edict that no one can pray to anyone but him for thirty days.

(It's a sad state of affairs when evil lights up your countenance)

Have you ever witnessed a worker of iniquity with a sly grin, or an outburst of a wicked laugh?

A grin lit up Kamur's face as he began to come into agreement with the plan of sabotage, synchronizing his heart to devise this wicked scheme. "I think we have finally got a plan," said Kamur.

(Private meetings with hidden motives and agendas)

Belok set up a meeting with the king. He orchestrated an opportune time for the appointment when he knew the king would be exhausted and easy to manipulate. Kamur, meanwhile, bribed the king's huntsmen to withhold food from the lions until further notice. On the appointed day of the meeting, the two governors presented their petition. King Darius upheld a brief

discussion questioning their motives; but tired to the bone –
as the two governors had predicted, signed the edict. It was
entered into the records of the kingdom, which accordingly
to the laws of the Medes and Persians could not be altered or
rescinded, even by the king.

*(God hates a heart that devises evil and feet that are swift in
running into mischief)*

Daniel, fully aware of the implications, entered his
private chambers, and kept right on kneeling in prayer to
God. The following morning, the conspirators were waiting at
the entrance of the throne room when King Darius arrived.
Belok, pretending he was sorry for having to report the
following news: "Oh my king, how deeply I regret that I must
be the bearer of disturbing news. The ink on yesterday's edict
is hardly dry, and already a violator has been discovered."
"Who is it?" the king asked. "I – I can hardly say it, for he
is someone you love and trust" After a pause, he went on.
"The violator is Daniel, my lord. Obviously, he has no regard
for your authority."

*(Don't fret. God has your enemies on His to do list. The Lord is
laughing, for he seeth that the wicked's day is coming. Psalm
37:12)*

The king fought to control his regret and grief and fury –
regret that he'd signed such a foolish edict, grief of the fate he'd
unwittingly imposed on his friend, and fury because he could
now see the conspirator's scheme. Darius called for his lawyers.
He pressed them to find some obscure point of the law allowing
edicts to be rescinded. But the lawyers assured him that no such
provision existed. In desperation, the king began to propose any
scheme that came to mind that might save Daniel all of which
were quickly rejected.

(The enemy putting on "The Squeeze")

Belok and Kamur came to report to the king that Daniel's
execution had not yet occurred. "You know, my king, that the
law of the Medes and Persians allows no decree signed by the
king to be changed."

(The Enemy: "Aha We Got Him Now")

On the day of Daniel's execution, King Darius stood waiting
in the twilight near his tunnel, his face wet with tears. "Daniel,
my friend, I've made a terrible mistake. You're facing this ordeal
because of my foolishness. I pray that you will forgive me." "I do
forgive you my king. But save your prayer and offer it to the God
of heaven on my behalf." "Yes, I will pray that your God will
deliver you from the mouths of the lions."

(Be Still and Know that He is God)

The guards escorted Daniel to the pit. He went with his head held high without resistance. They eased him into the shaft and released him. Immediately the roars grew frenzied with vicious snarls as the lions fought to be the first to reach the morsel when it hit the floor.

(God is a Mighty Deliverer)

The king, with his head down, returned to the palace, refusing to eat or comforted. For the first time in his life, the foreign king fell on his face and prayed to the God of the Jews – the God who had no image, no face, and no name but I AM. He prayed on his face. He prayed on his knees. He prayed while pacing around his bedchamber.

Very early the next morning, Darius hurried to the lions' den. "Daniel! Daniel!" He peered into the shaft. "Has your God delivered you from the lions?" "He has, my king. God's angel stayed beside me the entire night and turned those ferocious beasts into fawning kittens." Darius' heart soared, and words failed him. He ordered the guards to pull Daniel out. He had no marks from fangs, or claws anywhere on his body or clothing. The happy king put an arm around Daniel's shoulder, escorted him to his chariot, and drove him back to the palace.

(The Lord will cause the Tongue of Your Enemies to Stutter and Cleave to the Roof of Their Mouth!)

Soon thereafter, King Darius ascended his throne and ordered Belok and Kamur brought to him. King Darius said, "Since you were so eager to serve me in the matter of ridding the kingdom of Daniel, I thought it only fitting to show you what remains of his body as a memorial of your service."

"Oh no my king. No such token is necessary. We were only too happy to protect your throne from that troublesome Jew."

"Oh, I insist," the king responded. "It will be my pleasure to show you. Captain, please bring in the body of Daniel.

The two men turned as the captain opened the door and Daniel stepped inside. Their jaws dropped, and their eyes widened in terror. "How – oh how is this possible?" Kamur cried. "We saw him thrust into the den. We heard the lions fighting over him."

(Never Underestimate a Praying Man or Woman of God!)

"Daniel's God saved him from the lions," Darius said. "Now, we will see if your gods can save you. Captain, escort these manipulators and their families to the den of lions and cast them into it." "No! Please, my king! Belok shrieked. "We were only trying to do you good. Perhaps we were mistaken." They begged and pleaded; but the king didn't respond. They fell on their face before the king. "Please! Anything but the lions' den." Darius finally looked up. "I'm sorry, but I can't do that." He held up the parchment that he had written. "You see, I have already written the decree, and according to the law of the Medes and Persians, it cannot be rescinded."

Your enemies' condemning words will surely backfire on them!

WON'T HE DO IT!!!

The two men were dragged from the kings' presence and executed. The captain reported "Not one of them even reached the floor of the den, my king. The lions were raging at the base of the hole, tearing flesh and snapping bones. You'd think they hadn't been fed in a week."

The king made a decree that in every dominion of my kingdom men must tremble and fear before the God of Daniel. For he is the living God, steadfast forever; His kingdom is the one which shall not be destroyed, and His dominion shall endure to the end.

Darius didn't replace his two governors. Instead, he reinstalled Daniel as prime minister over all the officials of the empire.

MY BACKSTAGE EXPERIENCE OF DANIEL

When the Enemy Comes In

It bears mentioning again that first and foremost you need to understand that when you come under attack that it is spiritual in source and nature. Many times, we are tempted to look at circumstances or people and view them as the enemy. They may be the tools of the enemy, but the enemy is spiritual, not physical.

- We should wholeheartedly embrace these character traits of Daniel: courage, integrity, loyalty.
- We must have Conviction to stand against Compromise.
- We need the Right Companions. We need friends who will have our back in prayer.

- We must have Calmness and Courage. Oh, how I love it that Daniel never panicked or overreacted in the face of opposition.

Often challenged at work to resolve conflicts and difficult circumstances that demanded immediate attention, with the help of the Lord, my demeanor remained one of cool and calm. I remained poised and peaceful as spectating workers of iniquity look bewildered as to how I wasn't frantically panicking trying to simultaneously juggle all that needed to be done. I had to cover multiple open routes, handle customer inquiries, shift schedules at a moments' notice to resolve vehicle issues, resolve unforeseen emergencies, and other factoring anomalies. I accredit it all to the Most High God. The God of Daniel. The Righteous Judge of the Universe, who will be a spirit of justice to the one who sits in judgment and a source of strength who turns back the battle at the gate.

The standard comes before the strength. It's important to understand this divine order. We cannot expect God to be our strength if we don't embrace God's standards.

Because we have a standard, we don't have to compromise between the gates.

Because we have a standard, we don't have to conversate with what God has given us the ability to crush.

Because we have a standard, we don't have to negotiate with that which God has called us to trample upon. Our level is above the serpent.

Beloved, God is the saving strength of His Anointed, and He is calling His Anointed to a higher standard in this hour.

Now, let's glance back to the subheading: **"When the enemy comes in, (comma)."** It will do us a great injustice in the OVERCOMER's renewed mind; if we simply by-pass this scripture study on Isaiah 59:19. Let's now view through the lens of God as to what actually happens when the enemy comes bombarding you. The cry is to "Raise the Standard" as the scripture reads:

So, shall they fear the name of the Lord from the west, and His Glory from the rising of the sun. When the enemy shall come in like a flood, the Spirit of the Lord shall lift up a standard against him. (Isaiah 59:19)

For years, many of us have thought and preached as such "when the enemy comes in like a flood, God's spirit will raise up and protect." No and again I say No! In-depth study reveals, the one who comes like the flood is the Spirit of the Lord, and not the enemy.

It's known that the Old Testament was written in the Hebrew language and had no punctuations. The punctuations were inserted by translators. The comma (,) was misplaced in this verse. How do we know? First of all, in Scripture, only God comes like a flood, and not the devil; *"Thou (God) carriest them (enemies) away as with a FLOOD..." (Psalm 90:6).*

Secondly, if you carefully look at it from the Hebrew words used in the verse, you'd know that it is not talking about the enemy's flood that try to destroy us and the Spirit of the Lord coming to lift a standard against him, but instead it is the flood of the Spirit that sweeps away the enemy and his works.

Isaiah 59:17 in the Jewish Study Bible says: that *Adonai put on righteousness as his breastplate, salvation as a helmet on his head; he clothed himself with garments of vengeance and wrapped himself in a mantle of zeal (17). He repays according to their deeds – fury to his foes, reprisal to his enemies; to the coastlands he will repay their due (18); in the west they will fear the name of Adonai, and likewise, in the east, His Glory. For He will come like a pent-up stream, impelled by the Spirit of Adonai (vs.19). Who comes like a pent-up stream?* **THE SPIRIT OF ADONAI.**

The Amplified Bible puts it like this, *".... when the enemy shall come in like a flood, the Spirit of the Lord will lift up a standard against him and put him to flight - For He will come like a rushing stream which the breath of the Lord drives." (Isaiah 59:19b Amp).* Who comes like a rushing stream? **THE SPIRIT.**

Put another way: It doesn't matter who or what stands against you, the Holy Spirit will rise like a flood from within you, and do a clean sweep of your enemies; and all of their wicked works shall be washed away by The Spirit who comes like a rushing, pent-up stream. OMG - Hallelujah! It is false to believe as I once naively and immaturely thought: Get born again, and you won't have to worry about having enemies, or facing problems.

Jeremiah 1:19 says, "...they shall fight against thee; but they shall not prevail against thee; for I am with thee, saith the Lord, to deliver thee."

That is letting you know that, whosoever raises against you is fighting a lost battle." Jesus Christ is our banner! His victory is our victory when we proclaim him as Savior and Lord in the earth we are raising the standard! Glory to God!

Exposing the Accuser

As Nehemiah persevered in the midst of challenges, here is clear distinction of satanic opposition and how to identify it. In Psalm 56:2 David feels that he is being hounded by lions.

Satan will surround us with people who distract us. You know there are people in your life whose main goal is to waste your time, distract you, criticize you or confuse you.

Every day I was confronted by such forces operating through individuals. On other occasions, there are those relatively close to you that will hinder you; and yet at other times people will blunt out directly attack you! My point is the enemy will use anyone! *"Be merciful to me, O God, for man would swallow me up; fighting all day he oppresses me".* *(Ps 56:1).* Sometimes the enemy just wants to crush your spirit and swallow up your purpose! The phrase "all day" is translated from a Hebrew word that means "all the time; the total of everything." Literally it means that Satan attacks the totality of my life's purpose all the time! He is relentless. We have already learned of Satan's efforts to intimidate. *"All day they twist my words; all their thoughts are against me for evil"* *(Ps. 56:5)* Satan is the accuser! His goal is to slander, ruin and turn us away from victory. Satan will take what you say and do, fashion it into something that causes pain, and misrepresent you and what you believe! Psalm 56:6 declares that Satan stalks believers to hinder their faith. *"They gather together, they hide, they mark my steps, when they lie in wait for my life."* Simply notice that more often than not Satan uses people, even believers, to do his dirty work-life...In tracking through this psalm and others such as: (Ps 31, 32, 34, 35, 36, and 37) We discover the believers' victorious responses to the enemy and the response of our Triumphant Judge.

Politics in the Workplace

Just as I believe I was strategically positioned at my worksite location for the past years; I also believe there are those hired by the enemy known as hirelings that are also strategically placed.

The King James Version defines a hireling as one hired by the enemy. Let's also define some characteristics of "the hireling."

- John 10:13 -The hireling doesn't really have a pure heart; he's in it for himself," as explained by Jesus.

- Nehemiah 6:12- "I realized that God had not sent him, but that he had uttered this prophecy against me because Tobiah and Sanballat had hired him."
- Ezra 4:5 - A hireling seeks to frustrate purpose
- The hirelings - "bribed" officials to interpose delays and create difficulties, in order to hinder the work.
- Acts 8:9-11 - A hireling claims he has a superior knowledge of the Bible and a hireling claims his authority comes from God.
- Acts 8:12-20 - A hireling seeks power. A hireling likes to set doctrine and make changes that have nothing to do with your spiritual growth.
- Luke 10:7 - A hireling is only interested in creating a following. The hireling must be the leader.
- Matthew 6:24 - A hireling is loyal only to the organization he serves.

Working in different positions throughout my postal career serves as a reminder that in spite of the diversity, these experiences all had one thing in common: corporate business politics. Sadly, sometimes, no matter how well you do your job or how much time and effort you put into it, things don't always work out the way you want them to.

Even when you're minding your own business, over-excited vultures, out to make a name for themselves can mistake you for competition and bring you into situations that you never wanted to be a part of in the first place.

Before proceeding, it bears mentioning again that first and foremost you need to understand that when you come under attack that it is spiritual in source and nature. Many times, we are tempted to look at circumstances or people and view them as the enemy. They may be the tools of the enemy, but the enemy is spiritual, not physical.

Manipulation had been long set in motion by "the hireling(s)" at the onset of fulfilling a job vacancy position at my work location. The ill-intent (ulterior motive to demise, undermine) behind the flattery attempt to persuade the hiring official(s) to select them had been successful. The truthfulness and transparency of the interview process had been tainted and later disclosed as a "political move". Sometimes a person has political and relational skills that make them highly sought after or appear qualified more than what they really are.

It was official. The hireling(s) reported for duty; fully gung-ho into the new position(s). They show up on the scene to be seen.

Arriving with a lot of dazzling "bling, bling" of religious artifacts much like the Pharisees who displayed religion but no compassion. This was an excessive appeal. You don't have to rant and rave to display your "I love Jesus" outer garments all beaded and covered in rhinestones. When truly this does not reflect your inner man. There ought to be something identifiable, "a sure sign" about your behavior and demeanor that alone reflects the shimmer of God's Glory! When the (outer man) doesn't correlates with the (inner man), it is hypocrisy. It is also inevitable that the time of testing will reveal your true self.

The hireling(s) will always seek to study its direct competition, or the leader with the greatest influence, or the one fulfilling its desired position of prestige. The hireling(s) immediately set-up shop, working their way in becoming the (the go-to-person) the center of attention. I was pinpointed as one favored by God and indeed the one that hosted the most weight of influence. My extreme favor with the employees was a threat to hell's agenda. So, they quickly begin using the divide and conquer strategy by maneuvering to influence my colleagues and employees against me. Is any of this beginning to sound familiar? This was a direct attack in the area of my sphere of influence.

Immediately thereafter, I began sensing the impending heightened level of warfare. In this instance, I sought the strategic move of God through prayer. As I began to reflect on the Word of God, I was instantly reminded of Isaiah 41:8-16 and Micah 4:13. This WORD marks a defining moment for me as it so powerfully resonated in my spirit on March 15, 2010.

"But as for you, you are mine. Fear not, I am with you. Do not be dismayed. I am your God. I will strengthen you; I will help you. I will uphold you with my victorious right hand. See all your angry enemies lie confused and shattered. Anyone opposing you will die. You will look for them in vain and they will be gone. I am holding you by your right hand. I the Lord your God say to you – Don't be afraid; I'm here to help. Despised though you are, Fear not; for I will help you. I am the Lord your redeemer. The Holy One of Israel. You shall be a new and sharp threshing instrument to tear your enemies apart. By my divine direction and strength, you shall thresh upon the highest and strongest and most stubborn enemies. You shall thresh the mountains, beat them small, and shalt make the hills as chaff -And the whirlwind shall scatter them. (Isaiah 41:8-16).

So, Arise and thresh oh daughter of Zion... (Micah 4:13)."

It was as though the Lord was saying: This WORD serves as your signal of release by which to stand upon. It will be your weapon to use as you advance in the battles ahead. God will not leave us defenseless; and He is sure to cause the hidden realms to open up to us if we put our trust in Him.

Without first assessing or evaluating the current work culture or getting to know the personnel, the hireling(s) immediately began making more aggressive moves in disrupting the normal flow of the office work dynamics by attempting to persuade me in changing my processes, methods, and style of leadership - all in an effort to promote personal agendas. And when I refused to conform to their means and methods- they became more undermining and vindictive. They had come in wanting all control. The enemy's strategy is to put pressure on you from every side.

This methodology used by "the hirelings" was to remain undetected, so they began to initiate private meetings with upper management prior to each of our regularly scheduled supervisor meeting to release accusations, tension and hostility.

The lies of malicious whispers became malevolent roars over the next several months as they skillfully bewitched and manipulated the station manager and some of the other supervisors. A few of them rallied together forming an alliance against me and several others.

It's amazing how those you've worked well together with previously can so easily become negatively influenced and disconnected from you at the slightest gesture of untruth by someone barely known to them.

Negativity is contagious. Look out for its "carriers". Love them, lift them, but don't let them ever infect you. Learn to control the climate around you and filter what people say to you through God's Word.

At every meeting, the spirit of sabotage and hidden motives laced the atmosphere of the meeting room. It was a climate of distrust and deceit.

Are you able to recognize the source of such characteristics as previously discussed?

Through all the plots and intrigues that regularly lurked in such hostile climates, through all the jealousy that could only be expected toward positions of authority, through all the volatility and capriciousness, through all the envy, conspiracies, and persecutions, I continued persevering in prayer with the Word of the Lord before me.

Beloved, you best have on the full armor of God and the weapons of warfare at your disposal when entering such danger zones. It is the only surety of overcoming and quenching every fiery dart of the enemy while keeping your cool under fire when things get hot!

I've learned anytime light is being shined and a supernatural thrust is coming forth, there is always a counter punch and it will be an emotional swirl filled with rage, and resentment. Demon spirits will unleash accusation and offense as two frontline defense systems. They do this as a two-fold strategy. First, they are trying to avoid detection by misplacing the attention onto something that is not relevant. Second, they create emotional turmoil and distress so that the people rise against the voices of sound truth. This is a classical biblical pattern.

On occasions, the hireling(s) would walk pass and utter condemning remarks, and biblical phrases indirectly but within ear shot of me. One of which I distinctly recall was: "wolf in sheep clothing". It took great, great, great self-discipline on my part not to respond to any of these triggers.

I was so determined to honor God in my obedience to the strategy given me at the commence of this testing trial.

Like Daniel, God has called you to be a person not just of exceptional character, but of Christlike character – of Godly character. And like Daniel, He will take you into and through various trials to develop that precious, pristine character in you.

In the interim of everything that was going on, the hireling(s) carefully devised opportunities to approach me with small talk to gain my attention - alluding they had been prompted by God to give me a scripture to read or that they had a WORD from God for me. WHAT! I was like, "WHAT!" To myself, I thought "The audacity! Who does such a thing!"

On other accounts, there was one in particular at such time that focused exclusively on my work activities. I had committed no wrongdoing, but it was as if I was under satanic surveillance. My every move was being tracked. Have you ever noticed "on lookers," "spectators," or the creepy stalkers that thinks what you do is so easy or really so miniscule that anybody could do it? They think they're suitable to run circles around you until they are actually called on the carpet to fulfill standing in your shoes. The end result is they terribly fail, or they admit with hesitation "What you do is not as easy as I thought". The missing key is

You are graced in and for the assignment! You are favored by God to do what you do! In and of yourself, you too would terribly fail. But with Christ, you can do all things – because He supernaturally strengthens you, and His Grace remains sufficient for you.

Ironically, at this very moment in writing; Matthew 10:16 comes to mind. *"Behold I am sending you out like sheep among wolves. Therefore, be as shrewd as snakes, and as innocent as doves".* You must be wise as serpents! A cautious wisdom is necessary in order to deal with fierce opposition. In your thinking, be shrewd, but in your actions, be like a dove.

Within a few months thereafter, multiple charges of misconduct had been filed by others against the hireling(s) and they all were suddenly removed and reassigned. A swift vindication indeed!

During the testing period, the Lord God did not move out the enemy, but gave me revelation on how to proceed. The den of lions that was prepared for me, was the same den of lions that captured and swallowed the hireling(s). Likewise, just as God did not protect Nehemiah from the Samaritans' threats. He did however empower them to build while they were being harassed by the Samaritans. The message of Daniel, then, is not that God will remove all forms of oppression in our lives. Daniel was saved from the lions but not kept from them. In the same way God shut the mouths of the lions, He will shut the mouths of your accusers.

As Christians living in a fallen world, we can expect the wide-mouth, ferocious roar of temptation, intimidation, and scrutiny to snarl all around us. But when we put our trust in the Lion of the tribe of Judah, we do not need to fear any of them.

The God who delivered Daniel is the God who is able to deliver those who, like Daniel, believe in Him. The way to overcome it is to do nothing. *Romans 12:19 says; "Vengeance is mine; I will repay, saith the Lord."*

You say, "Do nothing!" Yes, sometimes you may be required to do nothing. "But I want to hit back when I get hit!" "I wanna snap off on somebody," Yeah, I know the feeling, and how well I know the feeling! But when we take vengeance, we hinder the Lord from doing His thing, whatever that may be. Believe me there were times when I actually could have retaliated from the injustices done. There were so many countless times I wanted to say something in defense of myself. But I had to learn to submit to the unfolding plan of God. The victory was not solely over my enemy. It was also for the benefit of me learning patience, humility, forgiveness, restraint and discipline in setting a watch before my mouth; keeping the door of my lips, and to trust God as my defender. In our anger, we often spew things from our mouth and do more harm than good. But it is our responsibility to discern the times to preserve our spiritual health and well-being. You will find in many instances; silence will be the greatest damage to the enemy's plans. The more you hold your peace, the more the power of God arises within you to show you how to win the battle. That is why, in the midst of the Israelites' complaints, Moses commanded them to hold their peace; God would fight the battle (see Exodus 14:14) So, Shhh and let God handle it!

Beware and Do Not Engage in the Warfare of "the Hireling."

The hireling(s) is hired by the forces of the enemy to pursue and provoke constantly. They can't stop or ease up because in a sense - they're being paid to torment and harass you. They always bring a heaviness that oppresses the atmosphere. They inflict destructive measures and further on down the road they don't even remember what they did. They later see you and start talking to you like nothing ever happened. They never say I'm sorry because they are clueless that they've been hired and used by the enemy. This is why you cannot afford to hold the offense of the hireling. You lose your effectiveness when you become offended. You must simply recognize who they are and the subtlety of their strategy and remain prayerful and focused on your mission and vision at hand. The Vision of the Lord will always prevail! You prove greatness when you overcome limitations.

Overcome evil with Good!

FIRE INTENSIFIED

COURAGE

Human societies vary widely in the things they value and the behaviors they honor, but they are all alike in one respect. They all admire courage. As Ernest Hemingway famously defined it, "Courage is grace under pressure."

But there's another kind of courage that is perhaps even more important. I like this statement about courage:

"Courage is necessary in many forms and in many situations, not merely in the extreme situations of war. We need it constantly, even if perhaps we are not aware of this. Every day, we must face things that threaten the good, we must face fear and pain constantly, and these situations always require fortitude." Courage in this sense is the strength to endure.

Faith On Trial

I chose to reference again the book of Daniel for my final backstage work experience; which was one of the most "fire-intensified" levels of warfare for me. In this lesson, Shadrach, Meshach and Abednego were willing to worship God even if He did not deliver them in the physical. They tell the king they do not need to defend themselves because God is their defender. They tell him that they are not concerned about the ability of their God, He is fully able to deliver!

But even if he does not, we want you to know, Your Majesty, that we will not serve your gods or worship the image of gold you have set up. (Dan 3:18 NIV)

Shadrach, Meshach and Abednego encouraged us in a boldness of faith to stand firm when the struggle is real, or real hot like in their case. However, it is this very stance of fortitude in courage and faith that gets them thrown into the blazing hot furnace. The fact of the matter is: even while displaying "unshaken faith," there are still struggles we will have to walk through.

This fiery furnace account continues in verse:19

Then Nebuchadnezzar was furious with Shadrach, Meshach and Abednego, and his attitude toward them changed. He ordered the furnace heated seven times hotter than usual and commanded some of the strongest soldiers in his army to tie up Shadrach, Meshach and Abednego and throw them into the blazing furnace. So, these men, wearing their robes, trousers, turbans and other clothes, were bound and thrown into the blazing furnace. The king's command was so urgent and the furnace so hot that the flames of the fire killed the soldiers who took up Shadrach, Meshach and Abednego, and these three men, firmly tied, fell into the blazing furnace. – Daniel 3:19-23 NIV

Ok let's stop right here.

That's a big pill to swallow for most of us. Because a lot of the prayers we want God to answer are good, noble and right. We want healing and increase and favor and prosperity. And we know if God answers our prayers as we want, we will gladly be willing to praise and worship and testify of His graciousness and goodness. I'm sure I'm right about that. But for now, let's cover all our bases. What if God's answer to our prayer is not what we wanted? What if the answer is no when we hoped for a yes? We cannot manipulate God. His sovereign rule is not based on doing as we please. He is God alone.

Now king Nebuchadnezzar does not believe that the God of Shadrach, Meshach and Abednego will be able to save them from his hands but as they previously made it known, "If God does not defend us here in the physical, if he does not protect us from the flames, we will still honor Him." Their faith was not conditional. They did not believe in the rescue, they believed in the Rescuer. They did not believe in the miracle, they believed in the Miracle Worker. They did not believe in the deliverance, they believed in the Deliverer. They were not looking more for the blessing than the One whom all blessing come.

Reality Check

Many times, we place these specifics on God. I'm blessed if I have a child by thirty, I'm blessed if I make 6 figures by 35, I'm blessed if I'm married by 25. But I can have all those things and still not be blessed if all you are doing is seeking what you want and not God. Seeking what you can get from the hand of God and not seeking the face of God. Do not get caught in this performance death trap of doing all these good things for God for the wrong reasons. The house, the car, the children, the spouse, the money, the American Dream is not your greatest blessing. God is!

The Fury Of A Fool

But when ole Nebby (Nebuchadnezzar) realized the bold stance they are taking he became furious and could hardly contain his rage. There were no more second chances.

"Heat the furnace!" he roared. "Make it seven times hotter than it ever was heated before!"

The servants ran to obey. Some started to throw even more fuel on the fire. Notice sometimes when you're down, everybody seems to wanna start slinging at you. Everybody wants a piece of you, even those you thought were your friends sink low to take a jab at you.

Now it was bad enough Shadrach, Meshach and Abednego were snitched on. It was bad enough they were summoned by the king and were threatened with the fiery furnace.

But now they are tied up to be thrown into the furnace. A furnace heated seven times hotter than before. I wonder if you've experienced the increased heat of temptation the bolder and more determined you are to stand for God?

Hotter and hotter grew the fire, until the king and the whole royal party could feel the heat of it. Now the problem arose as to how to get the young men into it. It was too hot. Nobody could get near it. Even the mighty men who had bound Shadrach, Meshach, and Abednego drew back, wondering what to do next. Throw them in!" yelled the king in his wild anger.

You Should Not Play With Fire

The soldiers obeyed. Picking up the three young men, they moved forward, threw them into the furnace. So high were the flames that the soldiers carrying out the order were themselves burned to death. Nebuchadnezzar did not care. He was making an example out of them for defying his authority. Nobody would dare disobey him again.

Never Alone

Fully clothed and bound, Shadrach, Meshach and Abednego are thrown into the fire. Understand this: Since God had already predetermined their end from the beginning, he already knew his plan of rescue for them. He could've very well put a stop to it all before they were actually thrown into the furnace. So why didn't He? Although God is faithful to save us from the fire, he will not always prevent the fire! Think about it. Could it be that the fire serves us a purpose?

The Psalmist even reminds is Psalm 23:4 *"Even though I walk through the darkest valley, I will fear no evil,*

for you are with me; your rod and your staff, they comfort me (NIV)."

We will enviably walk through some dark and difficult times in our lives, we will cross over some troubled waters, and will even pass through fiery trials; but rest to sure, we are never alone.

Let's continue reading at verse 24.

Then King Nebuchadnezzar leaped to his feet in amazement and asked his advisors. "Weren't there three men that we tied up and threw into the fire?" They replied, "Certainly Your Majesty." He said, "Look! I see four men walking around in the fire, unbound and unharmed, and the fourth looks like a son of the gods." – Daniel 3:24-25 NIV

Believe Not Only What You See

Holy Smoke...The fourth man seen in the fire with them is said by some scholars to be an angel sent from God while others believe that this man is what's called a theophany, which is a "manifestation of God in the Bible that is tangible to the human senses". Either way, God ensured that they were not alone.

When King Nebuchadnezzar sees Shadrach, Meshach and Abednego, he makes note that they are unbound and unharmed.

King Nebuchadnezzar sent them to the fire to punish them for not serving his god. He wanted his rage and jealousy satisfied at the expense of the destruction of their lives.

This account of Shadrech, Meshach, and Abednego proves that nothing or no one can separate us from the love of God.

Can anything ever separate us from Christ's love? Does it mean he no longer loves us if we have trouble or calamity, or are persecuted, or hungry, or destitute, or in danger, or threatened with death? As the Scriptures say, "For your sake we are killed every day; we are being slaughtered like sheep.") No, despite all these things, overwhelming victory is ours through Christ, who loved us.

And I am convinced that nothing can ever separate us from God's love. Neither death, nor life, neither angels, nor demons, neither our fears for today nor our worries about tomorrow – not even the powers of hell can separate us from God's love. No power in the sky above or in the earth below – indeed, nothing in all creation will ever be able to separate us from the love of God that is revealed in Christ Jesus our Lord. Romans 8:35-39 NIV

No flame, no fire, no struggle, no sabotage, no jealousy, no bullying threats, no word curse, no written curse, no witch, no warlock, no hireling, no jezebel. Not even the worst sins listed in Scripture, Nothing. Absolutely nothing can get between us and God's love because of the way that Jesus our Mater has embraced us.

Let's keep reading. Verse 26 says:

Nebuchadnezzar then approached the opening of the blazing furnace and shouted, "Shadrach, Meshach and Abednego, servants of the Most High God, come out! Come here!" So, Shadrach, Meshach and Abednego came out of the fire, and the satraps, prefects, governors and royal advisers crowded around them. They saw that the fire had not harmed their bodies, nor was a hair of their heads singed; their robes were not scorched, and there was no smell of fire on them. – Daniel 3:26-27 NIV

No smell of fire on them? Not only were they not singed, not only were they unharmed, but there was not even the evidence of the smell of smoke on them. That's what happens when God walks through the fire with you. Just as I share below another one of my experiences, you'll see as you go through a situation(s), people will never be able to imagine that you went through such an ordeal because God allowed you to come out unsinged, unharmed and still joyful and peaceful in your right mind. Hallelujah!

FIREPROOF PROVEN

In order for the fireproof to be proven, it requires following the order of God. Anybody can pray for their love ones or for others that they don't necessarily have an issue with; but the questions that I'm posing here are, "Can you pray in the spirit of fervency for your enemy? Can you travail for their deliverance? Can you cry out for Mercy on behalf of your hater?

Can you shift from your personal prayer of petition in a moment's notice and engage in warfare for the very one that lied on you, threatened to get you and has no remorse of the vengeful, hateful words they have spoken against you? Can you?

This level requires revelation, and divine obedience where you move in the precise timing of God. This requires you giving GOD your HEART. This level of maturity requires your complete yielding to the Spirit of God who is your Divine Helper.

Let me remind you right here: Upon the onset of the following situation, I'm still in the FIRE throughout all of these hellish situations and vicious attacks. But now, the heat of the furnace has just been turned up!

About two years ago during my prayer time and right after spending time in praise, I began meditating on the WORD, and the presence of the Lord filled the room. I knew at that moment something was about to "pop off"! I was instantly reminded to be dressed at all times in the full armor of God and to remain standing on the succeeding WORD (Isaiah: 41:10); as I was anointed with threshing power for the upcoming season.

The Lord was saying: "You know the drill. I'm teaching you new facets of prayer and war." I'm giving you teeth to chew (thresh) fresh, new meat. Justice will come, but justice will be delayed." I knew this was not the time to be venting with God about justice. It was a time for divine sensitivity and obedience for me to grow and develop spiritually. When God gives us a command, it is invariably rooted in our design. That means that I had within me the capability of doing whatever He was requiring of me. When God hardens you to difficulties; the things in your life that once seemed hard now doesn't faze you anymore in certain situations. This was another upgrade taking place in my prayer life. This was a "fire-proof" level.

When God shows up to do ground-quaking soul shifting; and you see the proclaiming of the Triumphant One fighting on your behalf, there will be no restraint as you scream the words, Victorious Overcomer to any and everyone!

The Holy Spirit went on to reveal to me the strongman that was influencing the life of this certain individual. As a prophetic intercessor, you are also called to be a spiritual sniper! God is counting on you to hit the target through your prayers. Also, as a true intercessor your heart cries for whoever you are praying for because MERCY is your true heartbeat.

Therefore, I did not hesitate. I did not give it a second thought! I didn't say let me process this a little later on today, nor did I say, let me first run all this pass my prayer partner. No. I got right up and went into intensive warfare. Threshing upon the strongman of fear and torment, rejection, bitterness, and unforgiveness. I commanded the strongman and its subordinate spirits to be uprooted. I called down the Fire of

God upon the spirit of Jezebel, I applied the blood of Jesus; and commanded every satanic altar and every high thing lifted against the knowledge of God to be snatched down by my horns of Iron. I trampled over and shredded them all into pieces with my hoofs of brass. This is Spiritual Warfare at the fire-proof level.

I then prayed for every vacated place of the enemy; to be filled with God's Love, Truth, Peace and Joy to superimpose over all the suffered hurt and pain of that person. I cried out for God's Mercy and Deliverance – that He would give them a wakeup call and that He would help them to let go and yield completely to Him. I prayed their hearts would open to receive conviction and truth. I prayed the Holy Spirit would stir a desire within their soul to want to receive freedom and manifested love. This prayer of intercession and warfare lasted quite a while. Praise God!

Later on, that same morning, as I was getting dressed for work, I wondered: "LORD, why would You have me to pray with such heart-felt fervency and tenacity for this particular individual?" There was no doubt He was well aware that this was the same one that treated me with such utter disrespect and contempt; set out to sabotage my workdays and falsely accused me at every opportunity given. The same one that despised me to my face, made blood-thirsty threats to one day get me, and indeed one day gritted their teeth with the expression of malicious hate and growled: "I! Hate! You!" Was I shocked? Yes. Was I hurt? Yes. Now, I ask you, "Have you ever been hated without a cause?"

After walking away from the office (the intensified heated fiery furnace) that day, I recall thinking to myself *what had I ever done to be hated so?* I immediately heard the words of Jesus, "The world will hate you just because you belong to me". I quickly realized that I wasn't fighting against a human figure; but against forces, authorities, rulers of darkness, spiritual wickedness in high places. I also knew this attack represented a faulty mindset that this person was holding onto without realizing the poison it carried. Some of the most common areas of attack comes through word curses and accusations from those who are hurt, offended, or just miserably misunderstood. I believed this was the case presented here.

People who have displayed a track record of this behavior are in need of deliverance. If such deliverance is refused, they need to be marked as strife causers. This is tough, but it is biblical.

Now I beseech you, brethren, mark them which cause divisions and offenses contrary to the doctrine which ye have learned; and avoid them. Romans 16:17

If you have ever been on the receiving end of these types of attacks, you know how much it will try to weigh on your emotions. The purpose is to steal your joy and zap your energy. Often times during a misunderstanding or disagreement, these things happen. It is vital that you, as a believer, are both quick to repent and also quick to forgive others. Let's remember that we all miss the mark at times; so, we need to be quick to extend grace to others in these situations, if they are repentant.

Nevertheless, I could not allow that poisonous venom that was spewed out at me to become embedded in me. I had to quickly declare the spiritual broom of Zephaniah 1 to sweep over my soul (which is my foundation) to purify me from the poison they released. I had to command every evil intent, every foul aroma to be flushed and be returned to the pit of hell and declare my foundational walls to measure up with the plumb line of righteousness. I had to pray like this to make sure my spiritual womb would not fashion deceit, nor house any type of retaliation, or bitterness.

You see, we must learn how to guard the anointing that's on your life, and Obedience is a pertinent key.

2 Corinthians 10:6 "....and being ready to punish all disobedience when your obedience is complete."

"Love your enemies, Bless them that curse you, Do good to them that hate you, Pray for them that despitefully use you and persecute you (Matt 5:44)"; and then leave the outcome of their lives in the hand of the Lord.

You may not always see immediate results in the natural; but you can have peace in knowing that you have done your part and God will most definitely do His. You can't waste time getting caught up in the darkness of those who refuse help. We must be about what God has called us to do and not look to punish those that hurt us.

Daily, at work, I am insulted by someone. At the same token I know that they have caused a blessing to fall on me and whether they acknowledge it or not, they bless me when they hate me or call me names. So, you should actually thank that special person in your life who is constantly insulting you because this is the result for you: *"If you are insulted for the name of Christ, you are blessed, because the Spirit of Glory and of God rests upon you" (I Peter 4:14)*

Trials humble us and develop character! There can be no *testimony* without a *test*; and if you don't pass the test, guess what? You get to take it again in God's Kingdom.

I now see how things have truly worked out for my good. There has been leanness and refines developed in my soul. Well Minister, tell us before the end of the book.

Did they ever come and apologize to you? "NO". The standard of the world will now say: "You mean to tell me, that you did all that praying like that; interceding, travailing, warring, crying out for mercy, all that for an enemy? Oh No! That does not make any sense! That is absolutely crazy! The devil's making a fool out of you. That is definitely not my swag"!

Well, I beg to differ because the Word of God declares "My thoughts are not your thoughts, neither are your ways my ways, saith the Lord" (Isaiah 55:8) Besides, how much stuff are you gonna continue missing out on because you're waiting on an apology from someone? Are you gonna suspend living until you receive an apology? Don't waste time because you may never receive that apology. Personally, I refuse to give that much power to a nobody. And what kind of an anointing is it when you pick and choose by personality if you like somebody or not, or if they're in good graces with you determines if you will pray for them or not. If that's what you're basing it on…. That's your personal ministry. That's not God's Ministry. That is not reflective of the Kingdom of God. That is not the lifestyle of an Overcomer.

Listen, God has to allow the enemy to manifest himself; so, you can see him for who he truly is; and that's what happened on that day. Only the Spirit of the Lord can reveal the concealed enemy!

There is so much more revelation that came forth from this experience but for the purpose of OVERCOMING, let me reemphasize this point in the light of obedience:

Sometimes you may not see the direct result of your overcoming acts of obedience. God often uses you in ways and plans that are bigger than you can understand or longer than you will live. God gives in His time, not yours or mine. We're not called to witness the results; we're only called to overcome evil with good. To simply perform the good task set before us at the moment. When we have done everything in our power to establish and maintain peace and yet the other person is not willing to have peace, then God does not hold us accountable for the lack of peace.

QUALIFED....TO OVERCOME THE FIERY FURNACE

I now realize no one wants to go through the fire-especially at an intensified level! But sometimes we will, and I would much rather go through the fire with Jesus than all by myself. Because when Jesus walks with us the only thing we lose in the fire are the chains that tried to hold us down. Such as revenge, bitterness, resentment, and unforgiveness. That is why to this day, I still pray for those demonically plagued by Jezebel, the hireling(s), the character assassinators, and the false accusers with much fervency, mercy and humility. Keeping in mind that we all have faults and shortcomings of our own.

BELOVED, DO NOT DESPISE THE FIRE

The three most inspiring things that I truly, truly, truly love about this testing trial:

◆ The Fire brings exposure to the hidden flaws in our soul and in our character.

◆ Just as God could've but chose not to prevent Shadrach, Meshach, and Abednego from falling into the flames, He could've, but chose not to prevent me from walking into those pre-sabotage meetings, and He could've, but chose not to prevent me from entering into the heated-up furnace of that room filled with poisonous venom.

◆ He will get you through your fiery trials proving that the very fire the enemy used to destroy you will be the very thing He will use to free, promote and bless us. You will OVERCOME ("walkthrough") the very same fire that will CONSUME others. Simply because once you've decided to serve God, to allow Him to be your defender, to trust in His ability and worship Him, and not the outcome, you will come out of any blazing furnace just as our friends Shadrach, Meshach and Abednego; unbound, unharmed and unshaken.

...And, that's what happens when God is with you in the fire.

CHAPTER 7

THE LION OF JUDAH ROARS IN ME

OVERCOMING PREMATURE EXPOSURE

"To everything there is a season, and a time to every purpose under the heaven" .... (Ecclesiastes 3:1)

In John 2:1-11 we see Jesus' family pressuring Him to prematurely expose His calling. Jesus understanding timing of seasons said: "My time is not yet...."

Being at the right place at the right time is conceivably the most ideal position to be in regard to opportunity, promotion and fulfilling your destiny. Regardless of what we think or perceive as opportunity, it must align with divine timing and God's designated process. The opposite of divine timing is premature exposure or wrong timing. This can cost you everything including your career, marriage, and even your life.

Premature exposure to political power, premature exposure to leadership (secular or Christian based), premature exposure to marriage and family, premature to money and wealth. Premature exposure of any aspect causes the seed to shrivel up when prematurely exposed.

If you give God the purging consent to sit upon the throne of your heart, He will indeed ALTER you on the ALTAR. He tempers the flame as He works good things into you and weeding bad things out at the same time. This is our personal Refiner purifying us. Whether refining precious metals or refining precious people, one point is certain: Purity is never achieved from only one firing in the furnace. Word of wisdom offered to you: Prematurely removing yourself from the ALTAR of sacrifice could be consequential costly! Allow Gods' working in you both to will and do of His good pleasure (Philippians 1:13)

THE MAKEOVER OF MY PERSPECTIVE

Changing your mind can change everything ....

"A pessimist sees the difficulty in every opportunity; an optimist sees the opportunity in every difficulty".

Please accept what I'm about to say. Some of you have sang the same ole song for so long that people are just sick and tired of hearing it. What do you think the Bible means when it says: Sing unto the Lord a NEW song? That means speak something out of your mouth besides the same ole thing all the time. "Poor me", "I'm the victim", "Nobody likes me",

"What about me", "I'm tired of being treated liked this", "I'm tired of this job".

Why are you crying the blues? Why are you in the dumps, dear soul? Why, my soul are you downcast? Put your hope in God, for I will yet praise Him, my Savior and my God.

We can do all the personal growth work we like, say affirmations, even meditate, but unless and until we change our thinking and perception, we are unlikely to have any lasting change in terms of a vast improvement in our quality of life.

I don't recall exactly when the shift in my perspective took place or when the adjustment in my attitude occurred; that I no longer viewed myself and workplace in the context of walking into a fiery furnace or onto a battlefield of a war zone surrounded by ferocious lions. Even though we are reporting to secular jobs, we are on duty for Him. God has a plan for each of our lives. My perception had changed. My perspective had been supernaturally recalibrated. It has to do with seeing through different lenses where light has been placed in the eyes of your spirit to function with 20/20 vision for correct understanding and interpretation of divine movements.

My new perception is "in Christ", and the flames I once fought are now the flames that I face because of a shift in my perception.

Those that fight the flames are characterized by: depleted energy, drained emotions, diminished joy, damaging accusations, dulled spiritual sensitivity

Those that face the flames are characterized by: an increased ability, a deeper understanding, a greater capacity, an acute realization, a positive outlook, a biblical viewpoint.

Our ability to maintain the right perspective allows us to finish well. The correct perspective enables leaders to successfully navigate tests, trials, and seemingly unfair circumstances. It gives leaders the ability to see God at work when it would be easier to jump ship.

RELATIONSHIPS has been a key indicator throughout this reading. Dealing with people successfully is the most significant factor in determining whether you will have the impact and influence you need to accomplish your mission at work.

Let me help Chaplains, Ministers, Preachers, Pastors, Men and Women of God who do not occupy a platform within the 4 walls of a church. Use your present platform well until God calls you up to higher ground. It's useless daydreaming about global platforms while you allow opportunities to use available local platforms pass you by. You should think globally but don't be ashamed to start small. Your pulpit is not necessarily with the 4 walls of a church building. It is wherever you're pulling others from the pit. My stand-up desk at work had become my pulpit.

God-honoring perspective at work. Few leaders have it...but it's a game changer in leadership.

MY SEASON OF STILLNESS

This season I spent recovering from a broken ankle.

Remember the SWORD that I had to use on myself in 2007? Guess what? As I was praying against strongholds one night during the writing of this project, I saw a sword to the right of me suspended in air. But this time thankfully, it was not to be used on me; but to be taken and used against the enemy. The Word of Thunder heralded in my spirit saying: ***"The Kingdom suffereth violence and the violent taketh by force"*** - "Take the Sword".

You know the potency of this sword. Carry the warfare into the enemy's territory, attack with the sword, for it is your calling, and thus will you best defend yourself. The best method of defense is an attack. "Take the Sword." Take it with a purpose and use it that you be able to stand and to withstand. "Take the Sword." Take it with confidence, take it with the grip of sincere faith, and use it in your holy war with full assurance, and nothing shall stand against you!!!

Since the time of the injury, I've had to regain my bearings in taking a different stance in declaring in the face of the devil "I know that every single thing you bring against me has been Father filtered; and you cannot do anything without God's permission. God edits out the trash that you are bringing towards me so that everything you bring at me is an opportunity for me to become more threatening to the kingdom of darkness as I master another dimension in the Kingdom of God."

Psalm 89:14 declares Righteousness and Justice are the very foundation of God's Throne.

Because of the great amount of injustices and difficulties you may yourself have endured over the past years; I declare this is a powerful season of repayment and justice. But understand it will not be automatic, you need to give your consent through prayer as you file your claim before the Righteous Judge of the Universe.

Listen, after learning that I had been replaced for the speaking event; I could have easily withdrawn and sulked, shut off the computer, slacked in praying, fasting, studying and all the necessary pre-work in preparing to minister the Word of God. But I remained active in keeping all of those things viable and as a result, the Lord added and increased unto me. We must not be found slothful; but faithful servants. Never mind if the enemy is present, you just continue moving forward.

My continuous moving is what serves the devil a "heel wrenching-crushing blow" signifying he is a liar, a defeated foe that cannot deter me! God steers my course!

As I stated in the preface of the book, this movement is about occupying territory. This is about the ground the devil has to give up; and he doesn't like it. As a matter of fact, he detests when you're unbothered and you're yet steadily moving and soaring to greater heights.

See ye then that you walk circumspectly, not as fools, but as wise, Redeeming the time, because the days are evil. Wherefore, be ye not unwise, but understanding what the will of the Lord is. (Ephesians 5:15-17)

We must get the wisdom and understanding of the Lord into what is happening... as the wisdom of man or this world will not work! Understanding Divine Timing is more than just showing up at the right time. It is a process of prayer, obedience, skill development, proper attitude, and discernment.

In this hour, there seems to be such a strong gravitational pull in the spirit on the people of God, a fierce force with a demand of "time" in the sense of keeping us preoccupied with busy stuff, running to and fro, from conference to conference, prophetic encounters, workshops, 6am prayer-line, 12 midnight shut in, 24 hr. Christian television programs, texting, tweeting, tagging, sharing post on Facebook and other social media platforms.

All of that is absolutely "good stuff" for some, but for the ones that God has CHOSEN and given divine instructions that are classified "time-sensitive" to accomplish specific assignment(s) – Be mindful. You cannot afford to be pulled in scouting and streaming you-tube all night long, searching the web for the latest up and coming events, or trolling Facebook postings.

You've been granted a window of space to complete your course; so, you don't have the time to be pulled here and there, tossed to and fro. Recognize, it's a ploy of the enemy to derail and distract you. He's attempting to cause you another missed opportunity. He wants you to miss out on accessing the divine portal that's scheduled for you. So, he'll keep pulling at you, drawing you away into those kinds of attractions. Those things your flesh seemingly gravitate to. Know that he doesn't mind if you're doing "busy stuff" or even "good stuff". Just as long as you're not doing anything "in obedience that's ordained by God".

Beloved, be wise not to become an addict to the point you're slipping and slithering in and out of conferences, and snooping and spectating on Facebook LIVE, recording and note taking from all these various platforms; yet not applying any truth to your life.

And although it may all well be classified "good" in nature; You should seek solely the Lord to increase your level of self-discipline that you will rise above the petty and fatal distractions of the age so that you can hear exclusively the intricate details of your assignment in this season. You are going to receive new revelation as God is going to open your book like He did with Jesus and reveal your assignment for this season.

As I'm nearing the close of this project, the following two scriptures come to mind:

"And Caleb stilled the people before Moses, and said, let us go up at once and possess it; for we are well able to OVERCOME it. (Numbers 13:30)."

"And they OVERCAME him by the blood of the Lamb, and by the word of their testimony (Revelations 12:11)."

By the blood of the Lamb, and the word of my testimony through this project demonstrates the STRENGTH and MIGHT of the Lord enabling me to slay some of the biggest giants, silence the roar of the accuser and overcome the furnace of affliction.... even from my place of stillness......

Now, that's how you OVERCOME warfare!

CONCLUSION

I DECLARE TODAY – YOU ARE AN OVERCOMER

(Job 23:10)
But He knoweth the way that I take "...I have the utmost confidence in him. Though I cannot see him, yet He sees me, and he knows my integrity; and whatever people may say, or however they may misunderstand my character, yet he is acquainted with me, and I have the fullest confidence that He will do me justice."

When He hath tried me -When he has subjected me to all the tests of character which he shall choose to apply.

I shall come forth as gold - As gold is for the application of heat and is thus tried in the crucible; the more intensified the heat is, the gold (our hearts and souls) comes forth purer and more luminous. Real piety will bear "any" test that may be applied to it, as gold will bear any degree of heat without being injured or destroyed. Thus, there is no danger of destroying true piety. It will survive the flames, and the raging heat that shall yet consume the world.

Beloved, think it not strange concerning the fiery trial, which is to try you, as though some strange thing happened to you. You are presently being prepared to possess greater territory even as you're digesting the final pages of this book. Testing is sure to come. Little did I know my hands were being trained for war and my fingers to fight; years prior to both my ministry assignment and workplace assignment. I was thrust into the realization that classroom time was over, and all of the on-going battles that led up to major wars had proved purposeful for training and development in the art of warfare. But I had to respond quickly to the awakening that it was time for action.

After being tried in the fire, you shall come forth as pure gold. You will also come forth with a greater anointing and testimony to inspire and encourage others during their fiery trials of life. So, hang in there and receive everything God desires for you and others in the midst of it.

Without consistently, showing strength and courage and imparting encouragement to those who follow you, you can pray, meditate and study the WORD of God, and ponder your vision night and day, but you will inevitably fail as a leader and a mentor.

However, a daily time of prayer and study in the Word of God, constantly keeping yourself in remembrance of God's revealed plan for your life, your family, ministry, or your business, and projecting the strength and confidence people need to see in you will bring great reward. As an Overcomer, you qualify to lead and mentor others through the challenges, difficulties, problems and even those fiery seasons of life – right into the center of God's Divine will.

Those in authority, ministers, businessmen, family leaders and future leaders, hear me LOUD AND CLEAR! Brace yourself and remember that not every door or opportunity that comes before you is from God. Not every promotion, elevation, blessing, or good gift comes from God. The devil also gives people gifts. However, his gifts are laced to distract the recipient from God's path for their life. It serves as a distraction to slow you down or to stop you from progressing. He said to Jesus, "All this I will give you," which means he as the power to give, but the devil never gives anything for free. He will make

sure that whoever receives anything from him pays dearly. So, hold fast, wait, and receive what is of God.
"For His blessings maketh rich and addeth no sorrow."
(Proverbs 10:22)

I pray you were blessed by the reading of this book which served as a source of encouragement to fight the good fight of faith on the battlefield where the majority of us spend most of our day – the workplace.

For I am thoroughly convinced this project was planted in me by God to display his GLORY and to declare Genesis 50:20 in the face of the enemy:
"As for you, what you intended against me for evil, (to harm me) God intended for good (to accomplish what is now being done, - the saving and deliverance of many lives).

It maybe generations later before the full impact of this project achieves the impact that God so designed; but you and I both know that the deal has already been sealed by Him. It is a finished work!

Today is a new day, a new start, a new chapter, a new beginning. This is your opportunity to make Jesus your LORD and SAVIOR, to align with GOD! Your experience, your college degree, your skills may not have taken you far, but the VOICE of GOD will take you far and above what you can ever imagine. *You, as an OVERCOMER are called to do something extraordinary!!!*

Start living a life of an OVERCOMER by making Jesus your LORD today!!!

Prayer of Salvation

"God, I want a real relationship with You.
I admit that many times I've chosen to go my own way instead
of Your way. Please forgive me for my sins. Jesus, thank You
for dying on the cross to pay the penalty for my sins. Come into
my life to be my Lord and my Savior. Change me from the
inside out and make me the person You created me to be.
In Your Holy name I pray. Amen"

"This is the victory that has OVERCOME the world; - our
faith. Who is he who overcomes the world, but he who believes
that Jesus is the Son of God?" (I John 5:4-5)"

INTEGRATE LADY WISDOM INTO YOUR WORKPLACE

The first step —----Start with GOD – only fools thumb their noses at such wisdom and learning!

➢ Angry people stir up a lot of discord, the intemperate stir up trouble (prov 29:22) MSG

➢ When there is chaos – everybody has a plan to fix it – But it takes a leader of understanding to straighten things out (prov 28:2) MSG

➢ First pride, then the crash – the bigger the ego, the harder the fall (prov 16:18) MSG

➢ God hates a heart that hatches evil plots, feet swift to run to mischief (prov 6:18) MSG

➢ God hates liars and those that soweth discord (stirring up trouble and strife) among the brethren. (prov 6:19) MSG

➢ God can't stomach arrogance or pretense; believe me, He'll put those upstarts in their place. (prov. 16: 5) MSG

➢ Among leaders who lack insight, authority abuse abounds. (prov 28:16) MSG

➢ A good leader motivates – doesn't mislead, doesn't exploit (prov 16:10) MSG

➤ God cares about honesty in the workplace. Your business is His business. (prov 16:11) MSG

➤ God can't stand deceivers, but oh how he relishes integrity. (prov 11:20) MSG

➤ God hates cheating in the marketplace; he loves it when business is aboveboard. (prov 11:1) MSG

➤ Mean-spirited slander is heartless; quiet discretion accompanies good sense. (prov 11:12) MSG

➤ Liars secretly hoard hatred, fools openly spread slander. (prov 10:18) MSG

➤ When a leader listens to malicious gossip – all the workers get infected with evil. (prov 29:12) MSG

➤ Slack habits and sloppy work are as bad as vandalism." (prov 18:9) MSG

➤ Listening to gossip is like eating cheap candy, do you really want junk like that in your belly?
(prov 18:8) MSG

➤ Escape quickly from the company of fools, they're a waste of your words. (prov 14:7) MSG

➤ A quiet rebuke to a person of good sense does more than a whack on the head of a fool (prov 17:10) MSG

➢ Don't ever say, "I'll get you for that" Wait for God, he'll settle the score. (prov 20:22) MSG

➢ Don't work yourself into the spotlight, don't push your way into the place of prominence. It's better to be promoted to a place of honor than face humiliation by being demoted. (prov 25:6-7) MSG

➢ Malice backfires; Spite boomerangs (prov26:26-27) MSG

➢ It's a mark of good character to avert quarrels, but fools love to pick fights (prov 20:3-7) MSG

MARKETPLACE PRAYER

BLESS THE WORKPLACE

God will be made manifest in the earth realm through my service, beginning now.

Heavenly Father bless my workplace as I consecrate unto You. Bless the works of my hands. Bless my relationships and all that I come into contact with today. I declare success in business today. Let my sphere of business be of great service to others, flourishing through decency, honesty and respect and honor for my colleagues and customers.

Because I have humbled myself beneath Thy Mighty Hand, You have exalted me to be a great light where darkness resides.
I have God-given influence in all governmental agencies, corporations, the education system, the medical industry, the field of entertainment, sports arenas, the media arena, Hollywood, the fields of modern technology and on Wall Street. I have favor in every endeavor of entrepreneurship that God sets my hands to pursue.

Heavenly Father grant me the supernatural wisdom of Solomon so that I can rightly access every situation and bring peace and productivity to the work environment. This wisdom allows me to prosper, be successful, and maintain godly priorities in my life. I will live a life to enjoy the work of my labor. This is my heritage from the Lord. Integrity is multiplying through my loins, and I am giving birth to a standard of doing business that will glorify God.

My success in the marketplace is not by power, not by might, but by the Spirit of the true and living God. My presence in the marketplace will add value to every person place, and thing I come in contact with. I will not despise small beginnings, and my latter rain will be greater than my former rain. God you are taking my business affairs from glory to glory.

Every demonic attack, spirit of distraction, and false prophetic word spoken over my business affairs are rendered null and void. The anointing of Nehemiah rests upon me and other servants of God in the marketplace. The ability to rebuild, restore, focus, conquer, guard and maintain good stewardship over that which belongs to God is upon me.

In Jesus name I pray. AMEN

ENDNOTES

Chapter

Wording

Resource/Reference

1

A small loss

http://bit.ly/39C37XO

1

The job of

http://bit.ly/36o7xQc

1

This scripture is

http://bit.ly/35jVgLk

2

I've been working

http://bit.ly/37ryxyc

2

In business, nobody

daydelotte@altavera.com

Chapter	Wording	Resource/Reference
2	Don't abuse your	http://bit.ly/2QJhEIz
2	The Law of	The 21 Irrefutable laws of leadership by John C. Maxwell
2	Not just to	http://bit.ly/2QJhEIz
2	Authority must be	https://revivenations.org/blog–Honor 1,2,3
2	when God calls	Book: The Point of No Return by Rick Renner (chaps 2,6,7)

Chapter	Wording	Resource/Reference

2

The weight of

http://bit.ly/2ZNYbKV

2

Marketplace Christians

http://bit.ly/2ZN4Ghh

2

Second Timothy says

http://bit.ly/2ZIDnES

2

This passage occurs

http://bit.ly/2SMFDJN

3

Millennials generally are

http://bit.ly/39IfPoi

Chapter	Wording	Resource/Reference
3	A survey by	http://bit.ly/2TdAc6O
3	Build skills -Mentoring	http://bit.ly/35qcuXg
4	As many tears	http://bit.ly/2FkvrAf
5	The character of	http://bit.ly/39GTO90
5	The fear of man	Book: Spiritual Warfare by Ron Phillips – (chap 16)

Chapter	Wording	Resource/Reference
5	Greed will also	http://bit.ly/2QHAD6u
5	The tool this	Book Spiritual Warfare by Ron Phillips (chap 10)
5	Jezebel is not	http://bit.ly/36rd1cX
5	A person can	http://bit.ly/36waFcE
5	In other words	http://bit.ly/2tyRKPR

Chapter

Wording

Resource/Reference

5

A sure sign

http://bit.ly/37zdmdO

6

If you have 2018

Unusual Vindication & Supernatural Justice

Apostle John Eckardt l Ryan Estrange l Rodrigo Zablah

6

To our understanding

http://bit.ly/2FkOY3G

6

Both Python and

2018 Unusual Vindication & Supernatural Justice

Apostle John Eckardt l Ryan Estrange l Rodrigo Zablah

Chapter	Wording	Resource/Reference

6

government corruption and

Book: Agents of Babylon by Dr. David Jeremiah (chap7)

6

So shall they

http://bit.ly/2MVxJKt

6

Satan will surround

Book: Spiritual Warfare by Ron Phillips (chap 34)

6

Vengeance is mine

http://bit.ly/2sLnEZz

6

"Courage is necessary

http://bit.ly/37zVyiD

Chapter	Wording	Resource/Reference

6

Shadrach,Meshach and

http://bit.ly/35jbPac

7

Being at the

Book: Divine Timing by Bishop Duncan-Williams

7

Our ability to

http://bit.ly/2ubHZaG

Conclusion

But He knoweth

http://bit.ly/2FkPDlG

ABOUT THE AUTHOR

Dr. Chaplain Brenda Bannister is an intelligent, classy and

 sassy woman of wisdom with elegance and excellence as her brand. She personifies this brand in all her endeavors. She's a rare sparkling gem.

Coming from a close-knit family, she relishes the opportunity to plan family gatherings, and is extremely family oriented. She allows her creativity to flow as she embraces the things around her and assists her mother in designing elegant gift baskets in her spare time.

Sometimes described as an extroverted introvert, she values her quiet time by reading and listening to instrumental music. However, she also enjoys shopping and her spontaneous lunch dates with her husband.

She's looking forward to retiring and traveling around the globe with her husband, and daughters.

For years, she's been fueled by her passion to give back to the community by visiting and praying for the sick at hospitals and nursing facilities across South Florida.

For the past 32 years Dr. Chaplain Brenda Bannister has sought to live a purpose-driven life as a devoted wife to her high-school sweetheart (Ernest); as well as mother of 2 beautiful adult daughters (Brenique and Brenisha) She is a devout instructor of prayer, inspirational writer, spiritual counselor, life coach, realtor, and a government civil servant.

She is a gifted kingdom leader whom God has entrusted to mentor, teach, and impact the lives of her many sons and daughters in fulfilling their destinies in the earth. She believes the marketplace and ministry have collided and now God's people are set poised to excel and operate in their true authority.

She is the President and Founder of Brenda Bannister Ministry Foundation, Inc., established to bring unity, intimacy and maturity to the Body of Christ. The heartbeat of this ministry functions as a Distributor of Wealth by adding value to individuals and ministries; in the equipping and empowering them to rise up in their true potential and fulfill their God's intended plan and purpose.

This no-nonsense, sought after prophetic voice is also known for shifting atmospheres as she releases an anointed distinctive sound of prayer that bears the weight of a mighty force in the realm of the spirit.

Of her many descriptive roles, the greatest role she plays in this life is that of a humble servant unto the Lord. As the crucifixion of "self" took place in her life - Intercession begun...and at this pivotal defining mark, she embraced the very essence of this honorable virtue: "After all has been said and done, my life's work must be rooted and grounded in servanthood with humility."

Dr. Chaplain Brenda Bannister

CONTACT ME

If you have prayed the Prayer of Salvation to receive Jesus Christ as your Lord and Savior; or if this book has changed your life, I would like to hear from you.

Please write me at:
Dr. Chaplain Brenda Bannister P. O. Box 15115
Ft. Lauderdale, Florida 33318 or
visit web: bannisterministry.org or
Email kingdomwealthdistributor@gmail.com

Made in United States
Orlando, FL
14 December 2023

40107103R00136